Library & Information Science
Objective Ability Tests
for NET/SLET/JRF

Library & Information Science Objective Ability Tests For NET/SLET/JRF

Suryakant

M.A., MLIS, Ph. D.
Chief Librarian,
Sampurnanand Sanskrit University,
Varanasi, Uttar Pradesh

and

O S Shekhar Singh

MLIS,
Librarian, Navodaya Vidyalaya,
Mewat (Old Gurgaon)
Haryana

Ess Ess Publications
New Delhi

Library and Information Science Objective Ability Tests for NET/SLET/JRF

ISBN : 978-81-7000-630-5

Rs.450/-

First Published 2011

Published by:
Ess Ess Publications
4837/24, Ansari Road,
Darya Ganj,
New Delhi-110 002.
INDIA
Phones: 23260807, 41563444
Fax: 41563334
E-mail: info@essessreference.com
www.essessreference.com

Cover Design by *Patch Creative Unit*

Printed and bound in India at Salasar Imaging Systems.

Dedicated

to

Our Teachers & Parents

Contents

Preface

Library & Information Science is a dynamic field of study. It is being taught in India an abroad on various levels leading up to Master Degree. It is one of the very important disciplines in the United Kingdoms, United State of America, India and many other countries of the world. More than 124 universities in India impart teaching up to Master Degree level besides the provision of Doctoral programmes. It has also been popular and useful as a professional subject.

Recently, the University Grants Commission (UGC) has evolved a method of selection and appointment at the universities by holding a National Eligibility Test (NET) for Lecturers in all the subjects and Assistant Librarians for the university libraries as well. Some state level universities also conduct the similar examination i.e. State Level Eligibility Test (SLET) for same purpose and these examination are recognized by the UGC and given equivalence to NET examination being conduct by UGC.

This test is held twice a year which universities conduct in June and December and Service Commission hold this test as and when vacancies occur.

The papers are held on the same day in two separate sessions. Paper I is compulsory for all of 100 marks having 60 objective type questions (in place of 50 questions earlier) and the candidate will have to answer 50 questions at their choice in this paper. Paper II and Paper III correspond to knowledge at the postgraduate level in Library and Information Science. Paper II is of 50 objective questions (Matching type, Multiple choice type, True/False, Assertion-Reasoning type) carrying 100 marks. Duration of these papers is 01 hour 15 minutes each. Paper III consists of only descriptive type of questions from the syllabus on the subject as described by the UGC.

Papers III will be of 200 marks and will have four parts, A, B, C and D. Part A will carry 25 marks and will have 05 text based questions (30 words) carrying 05 marks each. Part A questions test the critical thinking, ability to comprehend and formulate the concepts. Part B will carry 90 marks and will have 09 definitional/ short answers questions (50 words) carrying 10 marks each. The questions of Part B test ability to understand and express the same. Part C will carry 45 marks and will have 03 analytical/evaluative questions (300 words) carrying 15 marks each. Part C questions test ability to reason and hold an argument on the given topics. Part D will carry 40 marks and will have 02 essay type questions (500words) carrying 20 marks each. Part D questions test ability to dwell on a theme at an optimum level. The questions of Part A to Part D will be set from unit I to unit X. Thus, Paper II will be of 100 marks and Papers III of 200 marks.

Since it is a National Level Test, it is expected that the candidates possess comprehensive knowledge of the subject. In the first two papers questions are objective types. Every question has four alternative answers which are given just below the question.

Paper III is evaluated of only those candidates who obtain the minimum marks fixed by UGC in Paper I and Paper II.

The author of this book has covered Paper II only and it contains only objective type questions (Matching type, Multiple choice type, True/False, Assertion-Reasoning type) with answers given at the end of each page. There are six chapters in the book. It is strictly designed according to the New Revised Syllabus prescribed for NET/SLET/JRF examinations conducted by UGC and state level universities. All topics mentioned in the syllabus have been covered comprehensively.

It is hoped that this book will be help of those who are required to qualify objective test in subject and to get admission to Master's degree, M. Phil. and Ph. D. programme in Library and Information Science and requirement to various levels of library position at Colleges/Universities/ Government Organisations/ Lecturers in Schools and Department of Library and Information Science.

We express our sincere thanks and deep sense of gratitude to our teacher Prof M.T.M. Khan, DLIS, Bundelkhand University, Jhansi for his valuable guidance and constructive suggestions in bringing out this book.

We acknowledge with sincere thanks the encouragement and suggestions given to us by Dr. J. S. Burman, Lecturer, DLIS, Kurukshetra University, Kurukshetra (Haryana), Dr. G. C. Kendadamath, Assistant Librarian, Central Library, Banaras Hindu University, Varanasi and Mr. P. N. Sahu, PGT Physics, JNV Katni, and Mr. C.P. Ram, PGT Chemistry, JNV Nainital.

We are grateful to our parents who provided constant encouragement and moral support to complete this work.

We are extremely thankful to publisher Ess Ess Publications, New Delhi for taking their interest in the publication of this book and bringing it out in very short time.

The authors shall be welcome any suggestions for the improvement of this book.

Date: July 22, 2010

Dr. Suryakant

O. S. Shekhar Singh

1

General Questions

1. Library Science is a subject to study about:
   (a) Book Science
   (b) Science of book
   (c) Techniques & methods of library
   (d) Science of library
2. Library Science is an art or Science:
   (a) Science (b) Science & Art
   (c) Art (d) None of these
3. Which is the largest University Library in the World:
   (a) Delhi University Library, India
   (b) New York University Library, USA
   (c) Harvard University Library, USA
   (d) Bombay University Library, India
4. What was the name of librarian who was invited by Punjab University:
   (a) P. Charles (b) W. Borden
   (c) A. Pannizi (d) A. Dikinson

Ans. : 1. (c) 2. (b) 3. (c) 4. (b)

5. Who was the first Emeritus Professor in Library and Information Science in India?
   (a) P. N. Kaula (b) J. S. Sharma
   (c) D. N. Marshall (d) C. G. Viswanathan

6. 'National Library Week' is observed in India every year in the month of November:
   (a) True (b) False

7. Who founded the ILA?
   (a) Swaminathan (b) Ranganathan
   (c) Radhakrishanan (d) Vishwanathan

8. Where is the headquarter of IFLA:
   (a) Moscow (b) Washington
   (c) Paris (d) The Hague

9. Who was the first president of IFLA?
   (a) W. C. B. Sayers (b) S. R. Ranganathan
   (c) Issac Collijn (d) Melvil Dewey

10. J. Kaiser, J.E.L. Farradanne and E. J. Coates have made lasting Contributions to:
    (a) Classification theory
    (b) Cataloguing practice
    (c) Abstracting techniques
    (d) Indexing theory and practice

11. Directing user to the right source of information is called:
    (a) Digest Service
    (b) Referral Service
    (c) Data Service
    (d) Current Awareness Service

Ans. : 5. (a) 6. (a) 7. (b) 8. (d)
9. (c) 10. (d) 11. (b)

12. Public Law 480 (PL 480) is a/an:
    (a) Indian law (b) American law
    (c) British law (d) None of these
13. An individual who connects an internal colleague with an external source of information is a/an:
    (a) Information Consultant
    (b) Information Broker
    (c) Technological Gatekeeper
    (d) Information Intermediary
14. A. C. Wollner and M. O. Thomas were associated with:
    (a) Foundation of LA (b) Foundation of ALA
    (c) Foundation of ILA (d) Foundation of ASLIB
15. 'Content by Journal' is a kind of:
    (a) CAS (b) SDI
    (c) Routing of periodicals (d) Photocopy service
16. 'Tree of porphyry' is formed as result of:
    (a) Fusion (b) Polychotomy
    (c) Dichotomy (d) Decachotomy
17. The term UF (Used For) and SA (See Also) are used in:
    (a) Classification scheme (b) LCSH
    (c) LC (d) None of these
18. Who designated Dr. Ranganathan, as the father of library science in India:
    (a) Jawaharlal Nehru (b) Sir Radhakrishanan
    (c) Rajendra Prasad (d) Sir Maurice Gwoyer
19. Telecommunication is the transmission of information by electronic means.
    (a) True (b) False

Ans. : 12. (b) 13. (c) 14. (c) 15. (a)
16. (c) 17. (b) 18. (d) 19. (a)

20. Who is known as Dewey of Japan?
    (a) Fujio (b) Herohito
    (c) Sokteo (d) Anahito

21. Who is known as Ranganathan of Pakistan?
    (a) Dr. Khruseed (b) Dr. Hammed
    (c) Mohd. K. Khan (d) Mazid Ali Khan

22. Who is a female in the following:
    (a) Dr. Khruseed (b) Margaret Mann
    (c) C. A. Cutter (d) D. J. Foskett

23. Sadler Commission in India was setup in the year:
    (a) 1882 (b) 1902
    (c) 1917 (d) 1946

24. References and bibliographies are given while:
    (a) In data analysis
    (b) Conducting a research
    (c) Writing a research report
    (d) Conceiving a research problem

25. Xerography is:
    (a) Diazographic process (b) Dry copying process
    (c) Wet copying process (d) None of the above

26. 'Men are mortal, Raj is a man, Raj is mortal', this is an example of:
    (a) Seminal Research (b) Deductive Reasoning
    (c) Induction and Deduction (d) None of these

27. The word reprography means reproduction of graphic materials, irrespective of whether they are hand written, typed printed and so on:
    (a) True (b) False

Ans. :

20. (a)	21. (a)	22. (b)	23. (c)
24. (c)	25. (b)	26. (b)	27. (a)

28. Benjamin A. Custer edited:
    (a) LISA (b) AACR II
    (c) 19th edition of DDC (d) None of these
29. W ho was the teacher of Dr. Ranganathan in London?
    (a) H. E. Bliss (b) J. D. Brown
    (c) A. Pannizi (d) W. C. B. Sayers
30. Which honour was awarded to Dr. Ranganathan for his contributions in Library Science?
    (a) Gyanpith Award (b) Padam Shri
    (c) Padam Bhushan (d) Bharat Ratna
31 Who is the co-worker of Dr. Ranganathan in the following?
    (a) M. A. Gopinath (b) S. Dasgupta
    (c) P. N. Kaula (d) C. G. Viswanathan
32. The Open Access System was introduced in India by:
    (a) Ranganathan (b) Borden
    (c) Dickinson (d) P. N. Kaula
33. How many national libraries in Italy?
    (a) 4 (b) 8
    (c) 11 (d) 17
34. With which agency did UNESCO collaborate to establish UNISIST?
    (a) ICSU (b) IFLA
    (c) INIS (d) INFLIBNET
35. The concept of 'anomalous state of knowledge' was proposed by:
    (a) Ranganathan (b) Belkin
    (c) Lancaster (d) Vickery

Ans. :	28. (c)	29. (d)	30. (b)	31. (a)
	32. (a)	33. (b)	34. (a)	35. (c)

36. The concept of Technological Gatekeepers was first proposed by:
    (a) Allen (b) Guha
    (c) Diana Crone (d) S. M. Shah

37. MEDLINE on CD-ROM is published by:
    (a) UMI (b) AIU (India)
    (c) Cambridge Scientific (d) NLM (USA)

38. Who was Andrew Carnegie?
    (a) Information Scientist
    (b) Philanthropist
    (c) Teacher in library science
    (d) Librarian

39. In which year second Ph. D. was awarded by the Punjab University, India:
    (a) 1957 (b) 1967
    (c) 1977 (d) 1987

40. In which of the following universities Dr. S. R. Ranganathan did not occupy any post:
    (a) AMU, Aligarh (b) BHU, Varanasi
    (c) Delhi University (d) Madras University

41. Who was the first Chairman of University Education Commission in India?
    (a) Saroop Singh (b) S. R. Ranganathan
    (c) Dr. Radhakrishanan (d) C. D. Deshmukh

42. Since which year Dewey started the work for Decimal Classification:
    (a) 1868 (b) 1870
    (c) 1873 (d) 1876

Ans. : 36. (a) 37. (d) 38. (b) 39. (c)
40. (a) 41. (c) 42. (c)

43. IAC stands for:
    (a) Indian Academic Council
    (b) Information Analysis Centre
    (c) International Analysis Centre
    (d) None of the above

44. Information has become the most crucial weapon for acquisition of economic and political power.
    (a) True (b) False

45. U.G.C. was founded in the year:
    (a) 1952 (b) 1953
    (c) 1957 (d) 1958

46. UNESCO came into existence in the year:
    (a) 1944 (b) 1945
    (c) 1946 (d) 1947

47. In India the information products and service are marketed by:
    (a) NISCAIR (b) NASSDOC
    (c) DESIDOC (d) NISSSAT

48. Year that was designated as the Information Technological Year:
    (a) 1980 (b) 1982
    (c) 1983 (d) 1986

49. The model public library established in India with UNESCO's assistance was:
    (a) National Library
    (b) National Science Library
    (c) Connemara Public Library
    (d) Delhi Public Library

Ans. : 43. (b) 44. (a) 45. (b) 46. (c)
47. (a) 48. (b) 49. (d)

50. The Committee on 'Structure of Public Library Services in England and Wales' is also known as:
(a) Parry Committee (b) Kenyon Committee
(c) Roberts Committee (d) Edwards Committee

51. DRTC is not promoting research in the field of library classification.
(a) True (b) False

52. What is User's need?
(a) Books need (b) Information need
(c) Reading material need (d) Research periodicals

53. 'Book for all' is the same to which law of library science:
(a) Books are for use
(b) Every reader and his book
(c) Every book and its reader
(d) Save the time of the reader

54. In which year Dewey started the first School in Librarianship:
(a) 1856 (b) 1876
(c) 1887 (d) 1895

55. What was the name of the wife of Dr. Ranganathan?
(a) Sharda (b) Sarika
(c) Sushma (d) Sarala

56. India Office Library is situated at:
(a) Nepal (b) India
(c) USA (d) Britain

Ans. : 50. (c) 51. (b) 52. (b) 53. (b)
54. (c) 55. (a) 56. (d)

57. India Office Library Possesses the collection of:
    (a) MSS of India
    (b) Published in India
    (c) All published and MSS of India
    (d) None of these
58. Who was the first exponent of Scientific Method of Research?
    (a) Bliss (b) Newton
    (c) Bacon (d) Aristotle
59. Who devised the spiral of scientific method?
    (a) H. E. Bliss (b) C. A. Cutter
    (c) M. Dewey (d) S. R. Ranganathan
60. Writing system was invented by:
    (a) An ancient Egyptians (b) French
    (c) Greek (d) An ancient Indians
61. To find out the present Home Minister of India, appropriate source of information is:
    (a) Who's who of Indian Writers
    (b) Who was Who of India
    (c) India who's who
    (d) Dictionary of National Biography
62. Head of the University Library is:
    (a) Director (b) Deputy Librarian
    (c) Librarian (d) Chief Librarian
63. Head of the NASSDOC is designated as:
    (a) Director (b) Librarian
    (c) Chairman (d) President

Ans. : 57. (a) 58. (c) 59. (d) 60. (a) 61. (c) 62. (c) 63. (a)

64. 'Library is the heart of an institution', this was stated by:
(a) Dr. Ranganathan (b) Dr. Radhakrishnan
(c) M. A. Gopinath (d) Wilson and Tauber

65. IASLIC was founded in the year 1955 at:
(a) Bengaluru (Bangalore) (b) Chennai
(c) Delhi (d) Kolkata (Calcutta)

66. Who coined the term 'Information retrieval'?
(a) Lancaster (b) Faradane
(c) Colvin Mooers (d) J. Martin

67. The term 'News' 'Data' and 'Knowledge' are related to the concept of .... and thus are synonymous with the term.
(a) Information (b) Facts
(c) Both (d) None of the above

68. Who coined the term 'Informatics':
(a) Chernyi (b) Mikhailov
(c) Gilyarevaski (d) All the above

69. The barriers to communication and information flow are:
(a) Language problem (b) Economic problem
(c) Political problem (d) All the above

70. Non-verbal communication is categorized into:
(a) Three types (b) Five types
(c) Six types (d) Seven types

71. Today society consumes knowledge and information in:
(a) Developed society (b) Rich society
(c) Ablest society (d) All these

Ans. :

64. (b)	65. (d)	66. (c)	67. (a)
68. (d)	69. (d)	70. (d)	71. (d)

72. Credit goes to scientific policy resolution to:
    (a) Jawaharlal Nehru
    (b) Maulana Azad
    (c) Sardar Patel
    (d) Santi Swarop Bhatnagar
73. Mobile library is a kind of:
    (a) Small library (b) Public library
    (c) Extension service (d) Moving library
74. Library education in India was started by two Americans in 1911 and 1915 in the states of Baroda and Punjab.
    (a) True (b) False
75. The oldest and largest library association in the world is:
    (a) ILA (b) ALA
    (c) LA (d) SLA
76. The imperial Library was founded by:
    (a) Lord Mount Batten (b) Queen Elizabeth - II
    (c) Both 'a' and 'b' (d) None of the above
77. Name the Indian institutions offering Library and Information Science education for special libraries:
    (a) DRTC, Bengaluru (b) NISCAIR, New Delhi
    (c) Both 'a' and 'b' (d) None of the above
78. IASLIC (Indian Association of Special Libraries and Information Centers) is co-operating with:
    (a) INIS (b) UNISIST
    (c) NISSAT (d) All the above

Ans. : 72. (a) 73. (c) 74. (a) 75. (b) 76. (d) 77. (c) 78. (c)

79. Which of the following services are provided through indexing and abstracting service?
    (a) SDI service
    (b) Referral service
    (c) Document delivery service
    (d) Retrospective information service

80. KWIC indexing was devised by:
    (a) H. P. Luhn (b) D. Austin
    (c) C. W. Cleverdon (d) O. H. Kaiser

81. Which one of the following is not a part of the MARC record structure?
    (a) Directory (b) Leader
    (c) Check digit (d) Record terminator

82. ISO 2709 exchange format specifies:
    (a) The size of the magnetic tape
    (b) The tags to be used
    (c) A three-part record structure
    (d) All of the above

83. Dr. Ranganathan was the member of the cooperation committee of India with UNESCO during the period of:
    (a) 1945-55 (b) 1947-57
    (c) 1948-58 (d) 1949-54

84. Dr. S. R. Ranganathan was the President of ILA for the period of:
    (a) 1943-52 (b) 1944-53
    (c) 1945-54 (d) 1947-56

Ans. : 79. (d) 80. (a) 81. (d) 82. (b) 83. (c) 84. (b)

85. In the year 1965, Dr. S. R. Ranganathan was appointed as National Research Professor in Library Science in India.

(a) True
(b) False

86. Dr. Ranganathan started the designing of Colon Classification in the year:

(a) 1924
(b) 1927
(c) 1929
(d) 1933

87. 'Ranganathan as to Library Science as Einstein is to Physics', who passed this remark about Ranganathan:

(a) J. S. Sharma
(b) Pandey S. K. Sharma
(c) Krishna Rao
(d) E. Garfield

88. When did Punjab University start the publication of the periodical 'Modern Librarian'?

(a) 1910
(b) 1920
(c) 1930
(d) 1940

89. New Encyclopedia Britannica is published from:

(a) UK
(b) USA
(c) Canada
(d) France

90. Under which category of source of information Pamphlets are occur:

(a) Primary
(b) Secondary
(c) Tertiary
(d) Reference

91. The slogan 'Right book to the right reader at the right time' was given by:

(a) J. F. K. Drury
(b) S. R. Ranganathan
(c) S. S. Green
(d) D. M. Noris

Ans. : 85. (a) 86. (a) 87. (d) 88. (c) 89. (b) 90. (c) 91. (a)

92. Who coined the term 'Initiation of readers' first:

(a) E. J. Coates (b) C. A. Cutter

(c) Melvil Dewey (d) S. R. Ranganathan

93. Who used the word 'Bibliography' first?

(a) A. Brownson

(b) Calvin Moores

(c) Helen Brownson

(d) Louis Jacob de Saint Charles

94. Seymour Lubetzky is related with his contributions in the field of:

(a) Management (b) Reference service

(c) Cataloguing (d) Documentation

95. Who used the word 'Thesaurus' first in 1957:

(a) J. D. Brown (b) H. Brownson

(c) Dr. Ranganathan (d) Neena E. Browne

96. The term 'Information' was used in 1966 in USSR in place of:

(a) Documentation (b) Information

(c) Information Science (d) None of the above

97. Which name was given to Book Mobiles by Dr. S. R. Ranganathan?

(a) Book Mobile (b) Mobile Bus

(c) Librachine (d) Mobile information

98. Minimum, Midding and Maximum theories of reference service are given by:

(a) Samuel Rothstein (b) James I. Wyre

(c) Richard J. Beeler (d) S. C. Bradford

Ans. : 92. (d) 93. (d) 94. (c) 95. (b)
96. (c) 97. (c) 98. (a)

99. The basic elements of communication process are the source, message and the receiver.
    (a) True (b) False

100. Old and frogile books can be preserved by:
    (a) Microfilming (b) Digitising
    (c) Re-Binding (d) All the above

101. Budget is a:
    (a) Financial Method (b) Mechanical Method
    (c) Control Device (d) All the above

102. HRM stands for:
    (a) Human Regional Management
    (b) Human Resources Management
    (c) Human Research Management
    (d) None of the above

103. 'Functional elements of management' are known as:
    (a) POSTCORD (b) POASDCARB
    (c) PASDCARB (d) POSDCORB

104. 'Esprit de crops' implies:
    (a) Unit of command (b) Clarity of works
    (c) Avoiding of chaos
    (d) Rewards to employees

105. British Library Act was enacted in U. K. in the year;
    (a) 1948 (b) 1962
    (c) 1968 (d) 1972

106. Mark the odd in respect to library legislation:
    (a) Pondicherry (b) Delhi
    (c) Goa (d) Haryana

Ans. : 99. (a) 100. (d) 101. (a) 102. (b)
103. (d) 104. (a) 105. (d) 106. (b)

107. Which of the five laws implies weeding of books by libraries?

(a) Second law (b) Third law

(c) Fifth law (d) All the above

108. Which of the following public libraries act was passed in the year 2002:

(a) Mizoram (b) Goa

(c) Delhi (d) Uttar Pradesh

109. The alphabet used in Colon Classification- 7th edition to indicate partial comprehension (agglomeration):

(a) T (b) Z

(c) W (d) P

110. Which of the following is an Indian Network?

(a) ADINET (b) OPENNET

(c) MALIBNET (d) All of the above

111. The Association for Information Management was formerly known as:

(a) IASLIC (b) ASLIB

(c) SLA (d) None of these

112. Special Libraries Association (USA) was founded in:

(a) 1905 (b) 1907

(c) 1909 (d) 1915

113. Who is specialist of Information Economics?

(a) Lamberton (b) C. G. Jung

(c) S. C. Bradford (d) Derek de Solla Price

Ans. : 107. (c) 108. (a) 109. (b) 110. (d) 111. (b) 112. (c) 113. (a)

114. Which of the following is not a national library?
   (a) Bibliotheque Nationale
   (b) Smith Sonion Institute
   (c) British Library
   (d) Library of congress

115. Which of the following pairs is wrong:
   (a) Ranganathan - Chain indexing
   (b) G. Bhattacharya - POPSI
   (c) M. Dewey - PPBS
   (d) Paul Scalich - Encyclopedia

116. Time is very important factor between which of the following:
   (a) Reference & referral services
   (b) Short range & long range reference services
   (c) CAS & SDI services
   (d) Indexing & Abstracting services

117. Who started Reference Service in India for the first time?
   (a) W. A. Borden (b) A.D. Dickinson
   (c) S. R. Ranganathan (d) B.S. Kesavan

118. In which university library of India, the post of reference librarian was first created:
   (a) A. M. U. (b) B.H. U.
   (c) Delhi (d) Madras

119. British Council Library and American Centre Library come under the category of:
   (a) Public Library (b) Special Library
   (c) Embassy Library (d) Foreign Library

Ans. : 114. (b) 115. (c) 116. (b) 117. (c)
118. (d) 119. (a)

120. STPI (Software Technology Parks of India) is a society established by the Ministry of Information Technology, Government of India in the year 1991.

(a) True (b) False

121. What does INPADOC stands for:

(a) Indian National Patents Documentation centre

(b) International Patents Documentation centre

(c) Indo-Pak Documentation centre

(d) Indian Patents Documentation centre

122. Abbreviation ISO stands for:

(a) Indian Standards Organization

(b) International Standards Organization

(c) International Organization for Standardization

(d) None of the above

123. 22nd May is the date of birth of:

(a) S. Radhakrishanan (b) P. N. Kaula

(c) Raja Rammohan Ray (d) S. R. Ranganathan

124. Index Translationum is a big information source and bibliography of translated books published by UNESCO.

(a) True (b) False

125. NICMAN was established by NISSAT at :

(a) Pune (b) New Delhi

(c) Ahmedabad (d) Kolkata

126. National Information Centre on Management (NICMAN) is established by:

(a) NIC (b) NASSDOC

(c) RRRLF (d) NISSAT

Ans. : 120. (a) 121. (a) 122. (c) 123. (c)
124. (a) 125. (c) 126. (d)

127. MANLIBNET stands for:
   (a) Madras Library Network
   (b) Management Library Network
   (c) Mangalore Library Network
   (d) Mangoliya Network for Libraries

128. Who devised first bibliographic classification scheme:
   (a) Bliss (b) Harris
   (c) Bacon (d) Gesner

129. From which of the following words, the word Catologue is made:
   (a) Katalogos (b) Katalogus
   (c) Catalogus (d) Catalogos

130. The Barcode Technology was introduced in Library and Librarianship in 1972, when Kentish town branch of COMDEN Public Library began Plessey Light System for reading the printed code.
   (a) True (b) False

131. Who is the publisher of Encyclopedia of Library and Information Science?
   (a) Grolier (b) Mc Graw Hill
   (c) Marcel Dekker (d) R. R. Browker

132. A light pen is a/an:
   (a) Optical Scanner (b) Magnetic ink
   (c) Pointing Device (d) None of the above

133. ISBN has been accepted as official international standard in:
   (a) 1949 (b) 1959
   (c) 1965 (d) 1969

Ans. : 127. (b) 128. (d) 129. (b) 130. (a)
131. (c) 132. (c) 133. (d)

134. 'Book Bank' scheme of UGC was introduced in:

(a) 1959-1961 (b) 1961-1963

(c) 1963-1964 (d) 1963-1965

135. Which is the national Library of U. K.?

(a) The British Library

(b) British Museum

(c) London Public Library

(d) British National Library

136. The first President of IASLIC was:

(a) Dr. R. Chandra

(b) Dr. S. L. Hora

(c) Dr. Chattopadhyaya

(d) Dr. S. R. Ranganathan

137. H. E .Bliss was born in the year:

(a) 1817 (b) 1847

(c) 1867 (d) 1870

138. DDC - 21st edition was published in:

(a) July, 1996 (b) July, 1998

(c) June, 1997 (d) June, 1998

139. Who is generally the chairperson of the University Library Committee?

(a) Librarian (b) Pre-Vice Chancellor

(c) Vice- Chancellor (d) Registrar

140. MEDLARS - II started in:

(a) 1972 (b) 1975

(c) 1980 (d) 1982

Ans. : 134. (c) 135. (a) 136. (b) 137. (d) 138. (a) 139. (c) 140. (b)

141. Which laws of library science indicates that the documents of the library should be brought to the notice of users:
    (a) First law
    (b) Second law
    (c) Third law
    (d) Fifth law
142. 'No library is self sufficient in terms of its resources to meet the needs of its users' this statement leads libraries towards:
    (a) Formation of Library Committees
    (b) Library Cooperation and Resource Sharing
    (c) Enactment of Library legislation
    (d) Need for Management
143. A professional Association should primarily:
    (a) Work for the development of its members
    (b) Serve as an employment office
    (c) Function as a Trade Union
    (d) Undertake professional techniques

Ans. : 141. (c) 142. (d) 143. (a)

2

Information Technology and Library Automation

1. APINESS is:
   (a) NISSAT Project
   (b) ARPANET Project
   (c) UNESCO Project
   (d) NISCAIR Project
2. What does APINESS stand for:
   (a) ARPANET services in Social Sciences
   (b) Asia Pacific Information Network in Social Sciences
   (c) American Pilot Network in Sciences
   (d) Asian Pilot Project Information Network in Sciences
3. VIDIOTEXT system was developed by:
   (a) Microsoft
   (b) A T & T
   (c) IBM
   (d) CCITT & ITU
4. Abbreviation WWW stands for:
   (a) World Wild Web
   (b) Window Web World
   (c) Wild Web Work
   (d) World Wild Work

Ans. : 1. (b) 2. (b) 3. (d) 4. (a)

5. World Wild Web is initiated by:
   (a) IBM (b) NCST
   (c) ARPANET (d) CERN
6. The year of establishment of WWW is:
   (a) 1989 (b) 1992
   (c) 1993 (d) 1994
7. Telex is like teleprinter.
   (a) True (b) False
8. CERN is situated at:
   (a) Washington (b) London
   (c) Switzerland (d) New York
9. The word 'Hypertext' was coined first in 1965 by T. H. Nelson.
   (a) True (b) False
10. Abbreviation URL stands for:
    (a) Uniform Resource Locater
    (b) Unique Resource Language
    (c) Uniform Resource Language
    (d) UNESCO Research Laboratories
11. HTML stands for:
    (a) Hypertext Mark Location
    (b) Hypertext Markup Language
    (c) Hypertext Machine Language
    (d) Hypertext Mark Language
12. Abbreviation HTTP stands for:
    (a) High Transfer Transmission Protocol
    (b) Hyper Text Telecommunication Protocol
    (c) Hyper Text Transmission Protocol
    (d) Hyper Text Transfer Protocol

Ans. : 5. (d) 6. (b) 7. (a) 8. (c)
9. (a) 10. (a) 11. (b) 12. (d)

13. APINESS Project is related to:
    (a) New York (b) New Delhi
    (c) Paris (d) London
14. A database is nothing more than a computer-based record keeping system.
    (a) True (b) False
15. Abbreviation DEVSIS stands for:
    (a) Direct Education System for Science
    (b) Defence Science Information System
    (c) Development Scientific Information System
    (d) Defence System for Information Sciences
16. RECON is a/an:
    (a) Record retrieval services (b) Referral service
    (c) Off-line service (d) On-line service
17. RECON On-line technique is related to:
    (a) OCLC (b) NASA, USA
    (c) ARPANET (d) BLAISE, UK
18. Abbreviation RECON stands for:
    (a) Record Network (b) Retrieve Console
    (c) REmot Console (d) Research Continue
19. X modem was developed by:
    (a) H. Aiken (b) Chuck Forsberg
    (c) H. Hollerith (d) Word Chirstionsen
20. What does MIF stand for:
    (a) MARC International Formate
    (b) MARC Indian Formate
    (c) Machine Information Facilities
    (d) Mobile, Fax

Ans. :

13. (c)	14. (a)	15. (b)	16. (d)
17. (b)	18. (c)	19 (d)	20. (a)

21. Earlier name of OCLC is:
    (a) Ohio Computer Library Centre
    (b) Ohio College Library Centre
    (c) On-line Computer Library Centre
    (d) On-line College Library Centre
22. Y modem was developed by:
    (a) Howrd Aiken (b) Chuck Forsberg
    (c) Word Chirstiansen (d) Herman Hollerith
23. MNP stands for:
    (a) Micro Networking Protocol
    (b) Microsoft Networking Protocol
    (c) Microcom Networking Protocol
    (d) Multi Media Network Programmes
24. Who developed Microcom Networking Protocol?
    (a) Microcom Cooperation
    (b) Microsoft Co-operation
    (c) Softlink
    (d) CMC
25. UNIX is an example of:
    (a) System software (b) Operating System
    (c) Hardware (d) Database
26. UNIX Operating System is written in:
    (a) PL - I (b) PASCAL
    (c) C high level language (d) BASIC
27. The Internet is a world-wide network of computer networks.
    (a) True (b) False

Ans. : 21. (b) 22. (b) 23. (c) 24. (a)
25. (b) 26. (c) 27. (a)

28. National Centre for Supercomputing Application is also known as:
    (a) NACSA (b) NCSA
    (c) NCSUA (d) All the above
29. The first 'Data Network' was setup at Spain in:
    (a) 1971 (b) 1979
    (c) 1984 (d) 1987
30. Abbreviation NATIS stands for:
    (a) National Information Service
    (b) National Information System
    (c) National Informatics Service
    (d) None of the above
31. Under which organization NATIS functions:
    (a) UGC (b) NISCAIR
    (c) Department of Science & Technology
    (d) NISSAT
32. On-line Computer Library Centre is situated at:
    (a) Dublin, Ohio (b) New York
    (c) Washington (d) North Carolina
33. On-line Computer Library Centre is also known as:
    (a) Onclib (b) OCLC
    (c) OCLIC (d) None of these
34. CPM technique is used jointly to plan and control the process of long term projects in Library and Information Centre.
    (a) True (b) False
35. The year of establishment of OCLC is:
    (a) 1967 (b) 1971
    (c) 1973 (d) 1975

Ans. :

28. (b)	29. (a)	30. (b)	31. (c)
32. (a)	33. (b)	34. (a)	35. (a)

36. CSIR was setup in the year:
    (a) 1923 (b) 1932
    (c) 1937 (d) 1942
37. Abbreviation CCF(F) stands for:
    (a) Common Communication Formate (Fields)
    (b) Common Communication Formate (Factual)
    (c) Common Communication Formate (Foundation)
    (d) Common Communication Formate (File)
38. CCF - 1st edition was came in the year:
    (a) 1974 (b) 1984
    (c) 1985 (d) 1988
39. OPAC stands for:
    (a) Ohio Public Access Catalogue
    (b) On-line Public Access Catalogue
    (c) Optical Access Catalogue
    (d) Off-line Public Access Catalogue
40. What does ISBD stand for:
    (a) Indian Standard Book Description
    (b) Indian Standard for Bibliographical Description
    (c) International Standard for Bibliographical Description
    (d) International Standard Book Description
41. Windows - NT software was designed by Microsoft Cooperation.
    (a) True (b) False
42. SOUL software for libraries is developed by:
    (a) NISCAIR (b) Softlink
    (c) INFLIBNET (d) JNU

Ans. : 36. (d) 37. (b) 38. (b) 39. (b) 40. (c) 41. (a) 42. (c)

43. Abbreviation SOUL stands for:
    (a) Software for Universities Libraries
    (b) Software for University Libraries
    (c) Software for University Laboratory
    (d) Software for University Laboratories

44. The authorized distributor for CDS/ISIS software for libraries in India is:
    (a) NISCAIR (b) NCST
    (c) NISSAT (d) NIC

45. LSEase software for libraries is developed by:
    (a) AMU (b) BHU
    (c) LibSys Cooperation (d) INFLIBNET

46. What does LibSys stand for:
    (a) Library System (b) Library Services
    (c) Library Book Service (d) None of the above

47. Fax is a faximile machine:
    (a) True (b) False

48. Who launched the LibSys software for libraries in India:
    (a) UGC
    (b) NISSAT
    (c) NICTAS
    (d) NIC and Infotech Consultant

49. ENVIS is:
    (a) Discipline Oriented Information System
    (b) Problem Oriented Information System
    (c) Mission Oriented Information System
    (d) None of the above

Ans. : 43. (a) 44. (c) 45. (c) 46. (a)
47. (a) 48. (d) 49. (c)

50. Abbreviation ENVIS stands for:
    (a) Environmental Information Service
    (b) Environmental Information System
    (c) Environmental Network Information System
    (d) Environmental Network Retrieval System
51. ENVIS is situated at:
    (a) New Jersey (b) Nest West
    (c) New Delhi (d) New York
52. What does ADONIS stand for:
    (a) Article Delivery Over Network Information Service
    (b) Article Delivery Over Network Information System
    (c) Article Delivery On-line Information System
    (d) Advanced Network Information System
53. ISDS stand for:
    (a) International Serial Data System
    (b) International Standard Data System
    (c) International Standard Data Service
    (d) International Serials Data Service
54. Internet is an example of public network.
    (a) True (b) False
55. TECHNONET is located at:
    (a) Ethopia (b) Canada
    (c) Brazil (d) Singapore
56. PIS means:
    (a) Personal Information Service
    (b) Patent Information System
    (c) Patent Information Service
    (d) Project Information System

Ans. :

50. (b)	51. (c)	52. (b)	53. (a)
54. (a)	55. (d)	56. (b)	

57. Patent Information System is situated at:
    (a) Chennai (b) Kolkata
    (c) New Delhi (d) Nagpur
58. Under which organization ERNET functions:
    (a) Department of Electronics
    (b) Human Resources Development
    (c) Department of Education
    (d) Planning Commission
59. In which year Education and Research Network was setup in India:
    (a) 1985 (b) 1987
    (c) 1986 (d) 1988
60. Abbreviation CALIBNET stands for:
    (a) Calicut Library Network
    (b) Calcutta Library Network
    (c) Cambridge Library Network
    (d) Canada Library Network
61. The year of establishment of CALIBNET is:
    (a) 1985 (b) 1986
    (c) 1987 (d) 1988
62. Information and Library Network Centre is located at:
    (a) Ambala (b) NOIDA
    (c) Allahabad (d) Ahmadabad
63. EURONET is related to Europe.
    (a) True (b) False
64. UGC (India) is developed a library network:
    (a) ERNET (b) INFLIBNET
    (c) SIRNET (d) NICNET

Ans. : 57. (d) 58. (a) 59. (c) 60. (b) 61. (b) 62. (d) 63. (a) 64. (b)

65. INFLIBNET stands for:
    (a) Information Library Book Network
    (b) Indian Information Library Network
    (c) Information and Library Network
    (d) Indian Library Network
66. NICNET was established by Govt. of India in the year:
    (a) 1967 (b) 1973
    (c) 1977 (d) 1979
67. What does ERNET stand for:
    (a) Education and Research Network
    (b) Electronic Research Network
    (c) E-Research Network
    (d) Educator, Research Network
68. NICNET project (India) is sported by Government of India.
    (a) True (b) False
69. INFLIBNET was developed in the year:
    (a) 1976 (b) 1984
    (c) 1985 (d) 1986
70. Under which organization NICNET functions:
    (a) INSDOC
    (b) CSIR
    (c) Govt. of India
    (d) Human Resources Development

Ans. : 65. (c) 66. (c) 67. (a) 68. (a) 69. (d) 70. (c)

71. Abbreviation NICNET stands for:
    (a) National Information Centre - Network
    (b) National Informatics Centre - Network
    (c) New Delhi Information Centre - Network
    (d) New Information Chat - Network
72. CCF - II edition started in the year:
    (a) 1984 (b) 1988
    (c) 1989 (d) 1994
73. MARC II was introduced in the year:
    (a) 1967 (b) 1968
    (c) 1969 (d) 1971
74. CDS/ISIS software for libraries was written in:
    (a) BASIC (b) COBOL
    (c) PASCAL (d) PL-1
75. DIALOGE On-line service was started in 1970.
    (a) True (b) False
76. CDS/ISIS software for libraries was developed by:
    (a) UNESCO (b) UNIDO
    (c) UTLAS (d) UGC
77. Abbreviation UUNET stands for:
    (a) UK University Network (b) Unix User Network
    (c) University User Network
    (d) USA University Network
78. UNIX is a/an:
    (a) Operating System
    (b) Single user Operating System
    (c) Multi user Operating System
    (d) Network

Ans. :

71. (b)	72. (b)	73. (a)	74. (c)
75. (a)	76. (a)	77. (c)	78. (c)

79. UNIX Operating System was developed in:
    (a) 1959 (b) 1969
    (c) 1979 (d) 1989

80. UNIX Operating System was invented by:
    (a) American Telephone & Telegraph
    (b) Ken Thompson & Bell Laboratories
    (c) IBM
    (d) Tuplis Laboratories

81. UTLAS stands for:
    (a) University of Tamilnadu Library Automation System
    (b) University of Toronto Library Automation System
    (c) University of Tokyo Library Automation System
    (d) T.H. Nelson University Library Automation System

82. MS-DOS Operating System was developed by IBM in the year 1981.
    (a) True (b) False

83. MARC was initiated by:
    (a) ARPANET (b) OCLC
    (c) UNESCO (d) Library of Congress

84. MARC - I was developed in the year:
    (a) 1964 (b) 1966
    (c) 1968 (d) 1969

85. What does MARC stand for:
    (a) Machine Readable Catalogue
    (b) Machine Readable Classification
    (c) Machine Retrieval Catalogue
    (d) Machine Readable Code

Ans. : 79. (b) 80. (b) 81. (b) 82. (a) 83. (d) 84. (b) 85. (a)

86. DOS stands for:
    (a) Disc Operating Service
    (b) Disc Operating System
    (c) Digital Operating Service
    (d) Digital Operating System

87. Disc Operating System (DOS) was setup in:
    (a) 1979 (b) 1985
    (c) 1971 (d) 1981

88. DOS is:
    (a) Single User Operating System
    (b) Multi User Operating System
    (c) Multi Tasking Operation System
    (d) Language

89. Diskette is used in computer for data storage.
    (a) True (b) False

90. DARE is:
    (a) Software (b) Language
    (c) Referral Centre (d) Database

91. What does ITU stand for:
    (a) International Translation Union
    (b) International Telecommunication Union
    (c) International Telecommunication Unit
    (d) Indian Telecommunication Unit

92. MALIBNET stands for:
    (a) Medical Library Network
    (b) Madhya Pradesh Library Network
    (c) Madras Library Network
    (d) Maharashtra Library Network

Ans. : 86. (b) 87. (d) 88. (a) 89. (a)
90. (d) 91. (b) 92. (c)

93. Abbreviation DBA stands for:
    (a) Data Base Administrator
    (b) Data Bank Administrator
    (c) Digital Bank Administrator
    (d) Data Barcode Administrator

94. What does EDP stand for:
    (a) E-Digital Programming
    (b) E-Data Programming
    (c) E-Data Protocol
    (d) Electronic Data Processing

95. C-DAC stands for:
    (a) Centre for Digital Advanced Computing
    (b) Centre for Development of Advanced Computing
    (c) Centre for Data Analysis and Computing
    (d) None of the above

96. FRESS is a name of Hypertext system.
    (a) True (b) False

97. DARE database was setup by:
    (a) DELNET (b) DESIDOC
    (c) UNESCO (d) UNIDO

98. What is DIAS:
    (a) Disc Access System
    (b) Direct Internet Access System
    (c) Digital Information Access System
    (d) Digital Access Service

99. BLCMP (Project) was started in the year:
    (a) 1975 (b) 1976
    (c) 1977 (d) 1978

Ans. : 93. (a) 94. (d) 95. (b) 96. (a) 97. (c) 98. (b) 99. (c)

100. BLCMP programme is related to:
   (a) India (b) UK
   (c) USA (d) None of these

101. Abbreviation EURONET stands for:
   (a) European News Network
   (b) European Library Network
   (c) Europe Network
   (d) European Road Network

102. ComSet (project) was setup in USA in 1963.
   (a) True (b) False

103. EURONET - DAINE project was setup during the year:
   (a) 1978-80 (b) 1980-81
   (c) 1982-85 (d) 1983-85

104 What does OCR stand for:
   (a) On-line Computer Research
   (b) On-line Computing Research
   (c) Optical Character Recognisation
   (d) On-line Computing Rate

105. DNS stands for:
   (a) Data Network
   (b) Digital Network Service
   (c) Domen Name Service
   (d) Domen Name System

106. BRI and PRI are two standards for:
   (a) ISBN (b) ISDN
   (c) ISBD (d) ISSN

Ans. : 100. (b) 101. (d) 102. (a) 103. (a)
104. (c) 105. (d) 106. (b)

107. PRI stands for:
    (a) Programming Interface
    (b) Primary Programming Interface
    (c) Primary Rate Interface
    (d) Primary Rate Internet Service
108. FoxPro is a menu driven database management system.
    (a) True (b) False
109. Direct Internet Access System (DIAS) is developed by:
    (a) IIT, Mumbai (b) IIT, Madras
    (c) IIT, Kanpur (d) IIIT, Allahabad
110. Abbreviation ISP stands for:
    (a) Internet Service Provider
    (b) Internet Service Protocol
    (c) Inter Software Protocol
    (d) None of the above
111. NCST is situated in:
    (a) New Delhi (b) Kolkata
    (c) Mumbai (d) Chennai
112. CD-ROM audio version was developed in:
    (a) 1981 (b) 1985
    (c) 1975 (d) 1978
113. CD-DOD stands for:
    (a) Compact Disc - Digital Optical Diskette
    (b) Compact Disc - Digital Optical Disc
    (c) Compact Disc - Digital Optical Data
    (d) Compact Disc - Digital Data Output

Ans. : 107. (c) 108. (a) 109. (b) 110. (a)
111. (c) 112. (d) 113. (b)

114. Which one is the full form of NCST:
   (a) National Computing Software Technology
   (b) National Centre for Satellite Technology
   (c) National CD-Software Technology
   (d) National Centre for Software Technology

115. Punch Card is used as a data input:
   (a) True (b) False

116. BRI stands for:
   (a) Book Rate Information (b) Book Rate Intercom
   (c) Basic Rate Interface (d) None of the above

117. CD-ROM audio-visual version was introduced in:
   (a) 1983 (b) 1981
   (c) 1984 (d) 1985

118. CD-ROM digital version was prepared in the year:
   (a) 1983 (b) 1985
   (c) 1987 (d) 1988

119. What does CD-ROM stand for:
   (a) Compact Disc - Read Only Memory
   (b) Compact Disc - Read Only Memory
   (c) Compact Disc - Random Access Memory
   (d) Compact Disc - Read Only Mini

120. RDBMS stands for:
   (a) Reference Data Base Management System
   (b) Research Data Base Management System
   (c) Rational Data Base Management System
   (d) Info Research Data Base Management System

Ans. : 114. (d) 115. (a) 116. (c) 117. (a) 118. (b) 119. (a) 120. (c)

121. The year of establishment of DELNET is:
   (a) 1992 (b) 1989
   (c) 1986 (d) 1988
122. DELNET stands for:
   (a) Delhi Library network
   (b) Developing Library Network
   (c) Digital Library Network
   (d) Delhi News Network
123. That part of computer hardware, where programmes, instructions are interpreted and carried out, is known as CPU.
   (a) True (b) False
124. The first director of DELNET was:
   (a) Pandey S. K. Sharma (b) S. R. Ranganathan
   (c) Prof. Yashpal (d) H. K. Kaul
125. INDONET is situated in:
   (a) Kolkata (b) Mumbai
   (c) Ahmadabad (d) New Delhi
126. INDONET is initiated by:
   (a) IBM (b) CMC
   (c) NISCAIR (d) NISSAT
127. What does CMC stand for:
   (a) Computing Machine Cooperation
   (b) Canada Computer Cooperation
   (c) C Microsoft Cooperation
   (d) Computer Maintenance Cooperation

Ans. : 121. (d) 122. (b) 123. (a) 124. (d)
125. (a) 126. (b) 127. (d)

128. BLAISE stands for:
   (a) British Library Automated Information Service
   (b) British Library Association & Information Service
   (c) British Library Automated Information System
   (d) None of the above

129. Abbreviation IBM stands for:
   (a) Indian Business Management
   (b) Indian Bibliomatrics Machine
   (c) International Business Machine
   (d) International Bibliomatrics Machine

130. MS-Windows is an application programme.
   (a) True (b) False

131. What is ESS:
   (a) E-State Service
   (b) E-Serial System
   (c) E-State Software Service
   (d) Electronic Spread Sheet

132. Match the following:

(1) INDONET	(a) NISSAT
(2) BONET	(b) UGC
(3) ERNET	(c) CMC
(4) INFLIBNET	(d) Dept. of Electronics

   Answers:
   (a) 1 (a), 2 (c), 3 (b), 4 (d)
   (b) 1 (a), 2 (d), 3 (b), 4 (c)
   (c) 1 (c), 2 (a), 3 (d), 4 (b)
   (d) 1 (c), 2 (a), 3 (b), 4 (d)

Ans. : 128. (a) 129. (c) 130. (a) 131. (d) 132. (c)

133. DDE stands for:
   (a) Dynamic Data Exchange
   (b) Digital Data Exchange
   (c) Digital Document Exchange
   (d) Dynamic Digital Exchange

134. EWP means:
   (a) Electronic Word Processing
   (b) Electronic Word Processor
   (c) Electronic World Processing
   (d) Electronic Win zap Protocol

135. MS-Excel is an example of:
   (a) Hardware (b) Operating System
   (c) Electronic Spread Sheet (d) Modem

136. MEMEX hypertext system was developed by:
   (a) Boyles (b) Howard Read
   (c) T. H. Nelson (d) Vannever Bush

137. Match the following:

(1) FRESS	(a) V. Bush
(2) MEMEX	(b) A. G. Bell
(3) XANADU	(c) A. V. Darm
(4) Telephone	(d) T. H. Nelson

   Answers:
   (a) 1 (a), 2 (d), 3 (b), 4 (c)
   (b) 1 (c), 2 (a), 3 (d), 4 (b)
   (c) 1 (a), 2 (d), 3 (c), 4 (b)
   (d) 1 (b), 2 (a), 3 (d), 4 (a)

Ans. : 133. (a) 134. (a) 135. (c) 136. (d) 137. (b)

138. MODEM stands for:
    (a) Monitor - Display - Modulator
    (b) Modulator - de - Monitor
    (c) Monitor - de - Modulator
    (d) Modulator - de - Modulator

139. Telephone was introduced in the year:
    (a) 1866 (b) 1867
    (c) 1876 (d) 1877

140. ALGOL high level language is prepared in:
    (a) 1951 (b) 1957
    (c) 1960 (d) 1968

141 What is COBOL:
    (a) High level language (b) Machine Language
    (c) Spoken Language (d) All the above

142. COBOL high level language is introduced in:
    (a) 1940 (b) 1947
    (c) 1949 (d) 1950

143. What does COBOL stand for:
    (a) Common Business Orienthmic Language
    (b) Common Business Oriented Language
    (c) Computing Business Language
    (d) None of the above

144. Abbreviation ALGOL stands for:
    (a) A L Global Orienthmic Language
    (b) A L G Orienthmic Language
    (c) American L G Orienthmic Language
    (d) American L G Operation Language

Ans. : 138. (d) 139. (c) 140. (c) 141. (a)
142. (d) 143. (b) 144. (b)

145. Match the following:

(1) ALGOL	(a) 1940
(2) COBOL	(b) 1950
(3) FORTRAN	(c) 1960
(4) PL/1	(d) 1970

Answers:

(a) 1 (c), 2 (b), 3 (b), 4 (b)
(b) 1 (a), 2 (b), 3 (d), 4 (c)
(c) 1 (b), 2 (a), 3 (d), 4 (c)
(d) 1 (c), 2 (b), 3 (d), 4 (a)

146. FORTRAN high level language is developed by:
(a) Bell Laboratories (b) IBM
(c) TECHNONET (d) ARPANET

147. Abbreviation FORTRAN stands for:
(a) Formula Translation (b) Formate Translation
(c) Formatting Technique (d) None of these

148. WILSYS is also known as:
(a) Windows Library System
(b) Wipro Library Software
(c) Wipro Library System
(d) Windows Library Software

149. WILSYS is initiated by:
(a) Wipro Company (b) A T & T
(c) Softlink (d) NICNET

150. ARPANET project is sponsored by:
(a) U S Department (b) UNESCO
(c) U K Defence Department (d) NASA

Ans. : 145. (a) 146. (b) 147. (a) 148. (c) 149. (a) 150. (a)

151. The year of establishment of ARPANET is:
(a) 1946 (b) 1956
(c) 1960 (d) 1972

152. In which year RLIN was setup in USA:
(a) 1978 (b) 1983
(c) 1987 (d) 1994

153. RLIN is situated at:
(a) Dublin, Ohio (b) New York
(c) Scand ford, California (d) Net west

154. What does RLIN stand for:
(a) Research Libraries & Information Retrieval System
(b) Research Libraries & Information System
(c) Research Libraries Network
(d) Research Libraries & Information Network

155. SIRNET project was launched by:
(a) NISCAIR (b) DESIDOC
(c) NISSAT (d) CMC

156. Abbreviation SIRNET stands for:
(a) Scientific Information Research Network
(b) Scientific and Industrial Research Network
(c) Science Information Retrieval Network
(d) None of these

157. The year of establishment of SIRNET is:
(a) 1983 (b) 1987
(c) 1989 (d) 1991

158. Washington Library Network was started in the year:
(a) 1962 (b) 1972
(c) 1982 (d) 1992

Ans. :

151. (c)	152. (a)	153. (c)	154. (d)
155. (a)	156. (b)	157. (c)	158. (b)

159. Washington Library Network is located in:
(a) New York (b) Chicago
(c) Washington (Olympia) (d) California

160. The term 'Hyper Text' was first used by:
(a) 1965 (b) 1955
(c) 1945 (d) 1943

161. What is an IRC:
(a) Internet Re-connect
(b) Internet Reference Chat
(c) Internet Relay Chat
(d) Internet Re-chating

162. TCP/IP is a type of:
(a) Internet connection
(b) Network
(c) Programming
(d) Transmission Protocol

163. PDL stands for:
(a) Programme Description Language
(b) Page Description Language
(c) Print Description Language
(d) Personal Dialog Language

164. BLAISE is situated in:
(a) USA (b) UK
(c) Canada (d) Italy

165. Abbreviation TCP/IP stands for:
(a) Telecommunication Protocol/ Internet Protocol
(b) Telecom Protocol/ Internet Protocol
(c) Transmission Control Protocol/ Internet Protocol
(d) None of these

Ans. : 159. (c) 160. (a) 161. (c) 162. (a)
163. (b) 164. (b) 165. (c)

166. TLMS stands for:
    (a) Total Library Management System
    (b) Library Management System, Thailand
    (c) Thailand Library Management Software
    (d) Tata Library Management Service

167. Micro Computers were introduced in the year:
    (a) 1980 (b) 1985
    (c) 1988 (d) 1989

168. Digital Video Disc (DVD) was introduced in:
    (a) 1988 (b) 1992
    (c) 1995 (d) 1997

169. DVD-ROM was introduced in the year:
    (a) 1997 (b) 1998
    (c) 2001 (d) 2002

170. Digital libraries provide to access to digital information collections
    (a) True (b) False

171. PLEXUS is an expert system developed by University of Glasgow.
    (a) True (b) False

172. Hotbed is a popular search engine in the Internet.
    (a) True (b) False

173. The author of 'Multimedia Madness' is:
    (a) B. Atkinson (b) M. Goodwin
    (c) R. Wodaski (d) V. Bush

174. LOCAS means:
    (a) Local Catalogue System
    (b) On-line Catalogue System
    (c) Off-line Catalogue System
    (d) Local Catalogue Service

Ans. : 166. (a) 167. (a) 168. (d) 169. (b) 170. (a) 171. (b) 172. (a) 173. (c) 174. (d)

175. UTLAS project is initiated by:
   (a) University of Pune
   (b) University of Colombia
   (c) University of Toronto
   (d) University of Delhi
176. What does ADRS stand for:
   (a) Automatic Document Request Service
   (b) Automatic Data Reference System
   (c) A Document Request Service
   (d) None of the above
177. Match the following:

(1) ARPANET	(a) Govt. of India
(2) SIRNET	(b) U. S. Department
(3) NICNET	(c) INSDOC

Answers:

(a) 1 (a), 2 (c), 3 (b)	(b) 1 (b), 2 (c), 3 (a)
(c) 1 (b), 2 (a), 3 (c)	(d) 1 (c), 2 (b), 3 (a)

178. MEDLARS is initiated by:
   (a) NLM, USA (b) OCLC, Ohio
   (c) WLN, Washington (d) LA, UK
179. MEDLARS aim at catering information need of:
   (a) Science (b) Anthropology
   (c) Anatomy (d) Medical Science
180. MEDLARS stands for:
   (a) Medical Literature Analysis Retrieval System
   (b) Medical Literature Analysis and Retrieval System
   (c) Medical Literature Analysis Service
   (d) None of the above

Ans. : 175. (c) 176. (a) 177. (b) 178 (a) 179. (d) 180. (b)

181. 'Advances in Computer' is published by:
   (a) R. R. Broker
   (b) Macmillan
   (c) H. W. Wilson
   (d) Academic Press, New York

182. The frequency of 'Advances in Computer' is:
   (a) Monthly (b) Quarterly
   (c) Annual (d) Fortnightly

183. The first edition 'Advances in Computer' was published in the year:
   (a) 1960 (b) 1965
   (c) 1969 (d) 1975

184. MEDLARS was set up in USA in the year:
   (a) 1959 (b) 1964
   (c) 1979 (d) 1984

185. What is ASCII:
   (a) A code for information interchange
   (b) A code for information retrieval
   (c) A code for information service
   (d) A code for data interchange

186. What does ASCII stand for:
   (a) Asian Code for Information Interchange
   (b) Canada Code for Information Interchange
   (c) American Standard Code for Information Interchange
   (d) None of these

Ans. : 181. (d) 182. (c) 183. (a) 184. (b)
185. (a) 186. (c)

187. MIS stands for:
   (a) Management Information System
   (b) Management Information Service
   (c) Management Information Search
   (d) Master of Information Science

188. Which one is the full form of CPM:
   (a) Computing Path Method
   (b) Critical Path Method
   (c) Critical Programme Method
   (d) Catalogue Path Method

189. CPM technique is developed by:
   (a) Koontz (b) R. N. Anthony
   (c) Smith D. (d) Du Pont

190. Abbreviation PERT stands for:
   (a) Programme Evolution Review Technology
   (b) Programme Evolution Review Technique
   (c) Programme Evolution Re-print Technology
   (d) Programme Evolution Re-print Technology

191. UNIMARC is initiated by:
   (a) IFLA (b) UNESCO
   (c) NIC (d) E T & T

192. P C S means:
   (a) Programme Control System
   (b) Project Control
   (c) Project Control System
   (d) Personal Computer System

Ans. : 187. (a) 188. (b) 189. (d) 190. (b) 191. (a) 192. (c)

193. What does UNIMARC stand for:
   (a) Universal Machine Readable Catalogue
   (b) United Nation International MARC
   (c) United Nation - Machine Readable Catalogue
   (d) Universal Machine Retrieval Catalogue

194. Delpy method is used in:
   (a) Performance appraisal (b) Job evolution
   (c) Palmistry (d) For casting Trends

195. ISBD is initiated by:
   (a) OCLC (b) IFLA
   (c) UNIDO (d) ANSI

196. ISBN was developed in the year:
   (a) 1971 (b) 1977
   (c) 1979 (d) 1986

197. ISBD (M) stands for:
   (a) Indian Standard for Book Description (Monograph)
   (b) Indian Standard for Book Description (MARC)
   (c) International Standard in Bibliographic Description (Monograph)
   (d) International Standard for MARC

198. CCL stands for:
   (a) Common Command Language
   (b) Computer Control Language
   (c) Critical Command Language
   (d) Computing Command Language

199. Word 'Computer' Derived from:
   (a) French (b) Latin
   (c) Greek (d) None of the above

Ans. : 193. (a) 194. (d) 195. (b) 196. (a)
197. (c) 198. (a) 199. (b)

200. RENNIC is meant to offer network services to research, education and medical institutions in India:
   (a) True (b) False

201. D-Base is related with:
   (a) Keyword (b) Language
   (c) Programming (d) System Analysis

202. Microchip is initiated by:
   (a) IBM (b) Bell Laboratories
   (c) AVIS (d) INTEL

203. Central Processing Unit (CPU) is:
   (a) Heart of Micro Computer
   (b) Software
   (c) Information Retrieval Technique
   (d) Data Collection Method

204. CHECKMATE software is made for:
   (a) Circulation Control in a library
   (b) Data Analysis
   (c) Serial Control in a Library
   (d) Referral service

205. Software means:
   (a) Collection of instructions
   (b) Collection of programmes
   (c) Set of written programmes
   (d) All the above

206. System software means:
   (a) Collection of programmes
   (b) Set of programmes
   (c) Collection of instruction
   (d) None of the above

Ans. : 200. (a) 201. (c) 202. (d) 203. (a) 204. (c) 205. (b) 206. (b)

207. Plotter device used for:
   (a) Punching Paper Tap
   (b) Punching Magnetic Tap
   (c) Punching Cards
   (d) Punching graphs

208. Another name of Floppy Disc is:
   (a) Magnetic tap (b) Magnetic disc
   (c) Cassette tap (d) Diskette

209. Abbreviation RAM stands for:
   (a) Reference Access Memory
   (b) Random Access Memory
   (c) Read Only Memory
   (d) All the above

210. Bar-code labels are used in:
   (a) Reference
   (b) Serial Control System
   (c) Circulation System
   (d) Acquisition System

211. The fourth phase of communication is:
   (a) Written Era (b) Telecommunication
   (c) Printing Era (d) Mass Media

212. Face to face conversation is an example of:
   (a) Instant Communication
   (b) Infrared Communication
   (c) Protocol Communication
   (d) Distance Communication

Ans. : 207. (d) 208. (d) 209. (b) 210. (c)
211. (b) 212. (a)

213. What does NASSCOM stand for:
    (a) National Service for Software Companies
    (b) National Association of Software and Service Companies
    (c) Network Services for Software Companies
    (d) None of the above

214. Telestar project is initiated by:
    (a) A T & T (b) E T & T
    (c) IBM (d) Bell laboratories

215. ADINET stands for:
    (a) A Delhi Library Network
    (b) ARPANET - Digital Network
    (c) A Digital Network
    (d) Ahmadabad Library Network

216. MAITRAYEE software is developed by;
    (a) ADINET (b) CALIBNET
    (c) SIRNET (d) DELNET

217. MAITRAYEE software for libraries is initiated by;
    (a) LC, USA (b) UGC, India
    (c) CMC, India (d) Government of India

218. The third phase of communication is:
    (a) Printing Era (b) Written Era
    (c) Telecommunication (d) None of these

219. SANJAY software was developed by:
    (a) INFLIBNET (b) NISSAT
    (c) DESIDOC (d) INSDOC

Ans. : 213. (b) 214. (a) 215. (d) 216. (b) 217. (c) 218. (a) 219. (d)

220. Gutenberg was related to:
   (a) Verbal Era
   (b) Written Era
   (c) Printing Era
   (d) Telecommunication Era

221. UTP stands for:
   (a) Unshielded Twisted Provision
   (b) Unshielded Twisted Pair
   (c) Unshielded Transfer Protocol
   (d) Unshielded Twisted Protocol

222. STP stands for:
   (a) Shielded Twisted Pair
   (b) Shielded Twisted Protocol
   (c) Shielded Tele Provision
   (d) Shielded Tele-twisted Pair

223. Linkway Hypertext system was developed by:
   (a) AVIS Laboratories (b) IBM
   (c) Softlink (d) Microcosm

224. Linkway system was established in the year;
   (a) 1975 (b) 1976
   (c) 1987 (d) 1989

225. Match the following:
   (1) DELNET (a) Madras
   (2) ADINET (b) New Delhi
   (3) MALIBNET (c) Bombay
   (4) BONET (d) Ahmedabad

   Answers:
   (a) 1 (b), 2 (d), 3 (a), 4 (c)
   (b) 1 (b), 2 (a), 3 (c), 4 (d)
   (c) 1 (b), 2 (a), 3 (d), 4 (c)
   (d) 1 (b), 2 (c), 3 (a), 4 (c)

Ans. : 220. (c) 221. (b) 222. (a) 223. (b)
224. (d) 225. (a)

226. What does FRESS stand for:
   (a) Format Editing System
   (b) Format Entry System and Service
   (c) File Retrieval and Editing System
   (d) File Retrieval Editing System

227. Who gave concept of Technological Gatekeepers?
   (a) Diana Crane (b) Carolyn M Hall
   (c) L. W. Harrowded (d) Allen Kent

228. SRC stands for:
   (a) Sheet Reference Code
   (b) Subject Reference code
   (c) Subject Retrieval Catalogue
   (d) None of the these

229. Who was demonstrated the process of Microphotography :
   (a) Howard Read (b) M. Taube
   (c) B. Dancer (d) Frank Shepard

230. ALU and CU are part of:
   (a) CPU (b) CRT
   (c) CRD (d) Keyboard

231. What does CU stand for:
   (a) Computer Unions (b) Computing Unit
   (c) Computer Unit (d) Control Unit

232. Which one is the full form of Bit:
   (a) Bio-technology
   (b) Binary Digit
   (c) British Information Technology
   (d) None of these

Ans. : 226. (c) 227. (d) 228. (b) 229. (c) 230. (a) 231. (d) 232. (b)

233. Byte stands for:
   (a) Binary Eight Digit
   (b) Binary Digit
   (c) Both (a) and (b)
   (d) None of these

234. JANET is the programme of which country:
   (a) India (b) Canada
   (c) UK (d) USA

235. JANET stands for:
   (a) Joint Academic Network
   (b) Jail Network
   (c) Joint Asian Academic Network
   (d) Both (a) and (b)

236. The most popular vendor of online service has been DIALOG.
   (a) True (b) False

237. MAN is:
   (a) Network Project (b) Network technique
   (c) Structure of networking (d) Type of networking

238. What does MAN stand for:
   (a) Madras Network
   (b) Metropolitan Area Network
   (c) Mumbai Network
   (d) Maharashtra Library Network

239. Abbreviation PC - AT stands for:
   (a) Personal Computer - Applied Technology
   (b) Personal Computer - Application Technology
   (c) Personal Computer - Advanced Technology
   (d) Personal Computer - Advanced Technique

Ans. : 233. (a) 234. (c) 235. (a) 236. (a)
237. (d) 238. (b) 239. (c)

240. What is PC - AT?
   (a) A type of computer system
   (b) Programming language
   (c) A system software
   (d) A type of network

241. PROM is:
   (a) Output device
   (b) Memory
   (c) Language
   (d) Human bare

242. PC -XT stands for:
   (a) Personal Computer - Extended Technique
   (b) Personal Computer - Extended Technology
   (c) Personal Computer - Extended Topology
   (d) Personal Computer - Extension Techniques

243. Abbreviation WROM stands for:
   (a) Write Once Read Many (time)
   (b) Write or Read Memory
   (c) Write Once Read Once Memory
   (d) None of the above

244. What is DPI?
   (a) Digital Programme
   (b) Disc Per In charge
   (c) Disc per inch
   (d) Department Intercom

245. CRT is a part of:
   (a) CU
   (b) ALU
   (c) CPU
   (d) VDU

Ans. : 240. (a) 241. (b) 242. (b) 243. (a) 244. (c) 245. (d)

246. What does CRT stand for:
    (a) CODATA Referral Technique
    (b) Cathode Ray Tube
    (c) Control Technique
    (d) Control Technology

247. MINISIS is software for:
    (a) Computing
    (b) Information storage
    (c) Library automation
    (d) Word processing

248. MINISIS software for libraries is initiated by:
    (a) National Development Research Centre
    (b) National Informatics Centre
    (c) NISCAIR
    (d) IBM

249. IRDC is located at:
    (a) London
    (b) Paris
    (c) Canada
    (d) Scotland

250. DELMS stands for:
    (a) Defence Library Microsoft System
    (b) Defence Library Management System
    (c) DESIDOC Library Management System
    (d) DESIDOC Library Microsoft System

251. DELMS project was launched by:
    (a) NISCAIR
    (b) UNESCO
    (c) NISSAT
    (d) DESIDOC

252. LibSys is:
    (a) An application software
    (b) Menu driven software package
    (c) A library software
    (d) All the above

Ans. : 246. (b) 247. (c) 248. (a) 249. (c) 250. (b) 251. (d) 252. (d)

253. MINISIS software for library is set up in the year:
   (a) 1964-72 (b) 1968-70
   (c) 1970-72 (d) 1974-76
254. In computer, DTP stands for:
   (a) Digital Transfer Protocol
   (b) Direct Transmission Protocol
   (c) Desk Top Publishing
   (d) Digital Training Programme
255. ARPANET stands for:
   (a) Applied Research Project Agency - network
   (b) Advanced Research Project Agency - Network
   (c) NASA Project Agency - Network
   (d) A Research Project Agency - Network
256. Who used DTP term first?
   (a) Wyre and Rothstein
   (b) H. P. Luhn and G. S. Bonn
   (c) Paul Brainord and Apple Machintosh
   (d) Allen Kent and H. Lancer
257. What means WYSIWYG:
   (a) Wipro Library System for Windows Application
   (b) What You See is What You Get
   (c) Both (a) and (b)
   (d) None of the above
258. What does BONET stand for:
   (a) BIOSIS - OCLC Network
   (b) BARC Library Network
   (c) Bombay Network
   (d) Bombay Library Network

Ans. : 253. (d) 254. (c) 255. (b) 256. (c) 257. (b) 258. (d)

259. What is Topology?
    (a) A search technique
    (b) Structure of networking
    (c) Tool of networking
    (d) Characteristic of networking

260. BONET is developed by:
    (a) Planning Commission (b) CMC
    (c) INSDOC (d) NISSAT

261. CAI is a name of:
    (a) Software (b) Hardware
    (c) Programme (d) Language

262. Match the following:
    (1) SIRNET (a) LA (UK)
    (2) CARIS (b) AGRIS
    (3) AGLINET (c) INSDOC
    (4) JANET (d) NISSAT

    Answers:
    (a) 1 (a), 2 (b), 3 (c), 4 (d)
    (b) 1 (d), 2 (a), 3 (b), 4 (c)
    (c) 1 (c), 2 (b), 3 (b), 4 (a)
    (d) 1 (a), 2 (b), 3 (b), 4 (a)

263. Gopher is a File Transfer Protocol.
    (a) True (b) False

264. What is programme?
    (a) Collection of instructions
    (b) Collection of written programmes
    (c) Set of written programmes
    (d) All the above

Ans. : 259. (b) 260. (d) 261. (a) 262. (c) 263. (a) 264. (a)

265. In the context of computer, Virus is:
   (a) Language (b) Software
   (c) Programme (d) Hardware
266. One of the following is not a programming language:
   (a) BASIC (b) ASCII
   (c) COBOL (d) FORTRAN
267. A symbolically representing digits and alphabets through a series of bars is known as Bar Code.
   (a) True (b) False
268. Laser Technology is developed in the year:
   (a) 1949 (b) 1950
   (c) 1956 (d) 1960
269. PL/1 is a:
   (a) Low level language (b) High level language
   (c) Computer software (d) Machine language
270. ComSet stands for:
   (a) Computer Setup technique
   (b) Computer Set
   (c) Communication Satellite Technology
   (d) Communication Satellite
271. AGLINET is started by:
   (a) INSDOC (b) A T & T
   (c) AGRIS (d) ICAR
272. Abbreviation AGLINET stands for:
   (a) American Libraries Network
   (b) Agricultural Libraries Network
   (c) Agricultural Information Network
   (d) American Glass Libraries Network

Ans. : 265. (c) 266. (b) 267. (a) 268. (d)
269. (b) 270. (d) 271. (c) 272. (b)

273. What does CARIS stand for:
   (a) Current Agricultural Research Information System
   (b) Current Research Information System
   (c) Both (a) and (b)
   (d) None of the above

274. 'Lipi' is a dedicated word processor developed by CMC:
   (a) True (b) False

275. CARIS project is started by:
   (a) FAO (b) ARIC
   (c) ICAR (d) AGRIS

276. BLCMP stands for:
   (a) Birmingham Libraries Cooperation Mechanization Project
   (b) British Libraries Cooperative Mechanization Project
   (c) Bengal Libraries Cooperative Mechanization Project
   (d) Baroda Libraries Cooperative Mechanization Project

277. Cell phone is an example of:
   (a) Fiber Optics based Transmission
   (b) TCP/IP
   (c) Infrared Transmission
   (d) Microwave Transmission

278. Most friendly computer language is:
   (a) PL - 1 (b) COBOL
   (c) BASIC (d) FORTRAN

Ans. : 273. (a) 274. (a) 275. (d) 276. (a) 277. (d) 278. (c)

279. Who was the former chairman of UGC, first time proposal networking of libraries of universities and R & D institutions in India.
    (a) Prof. Yashpal (b) S. R. Ranganathan
    (c) V. K. R. V. Rao (d) C. D. Deshmukh

280. MS-Windows is:
    (a) Application Programme (b) Operating System
    (c) Software (d) Input devices

281. In EBCDIC, character represent in:
    (a) 4 bits (b) 5 bits
    (c) 7 bits (d) 8 bits

282. EBCDIC is:
    (a) A code for information interchange
    (b) A code for information processing
    (c) A code for information retrieval
    (d) A code for data analysis

283. Machine Translation means:
    (a) Convert programming language to machine language
    (b) Convert natural language to artificial language
    (c) Convert machine language to assembly language
    (d) None of the above

284. What does EBCDIC stand for:
    (a) E-Book Catalogue Digital Intet Code
    (b) Extended Binary Coded Digital Interchange Code
    (c) Extended Binary Coded Decimal Interchange Code
    (d) None of these

Ans. : 279. (a) 280. (b) 281. (d) 282. (a) 283. (b) 284. (c)

285. Flowchart is used in:
   (a) System analysis (b) Computing
   (c) Information retrieval (d) Programming
286. DAT stands for:
   (a) Digital Auto
   (b) Digital Auto Tape
   (c) Digital Audio Tape
   (d) Digital Audio-Visual Tape
287. Punch card system was popular in the libraries of countries during:
   (a) 1940's (b) 1950's
   (c) 1960's (d) 1970's
288. MS-Word is a part of:
   (a) MS-Windows (b) MS-DOS
   (c) MS-Excel (d) MS-Office
289. System boundaries are also known as:
   (a) System limitations (b) System setup
   (c) System analysis (d) System network
290. What is Sco-Zenix?
   (a) Database
   (b) System software
   (c) Single user operating system
   (d) Multi user operating system
291. First Disc Operating System was introduced by:
   (a) A T & T (b) IBM
   (c) INTEL (d) INFOTECH
292. A pre determined section of a record is called:
   (a) File (b) Data
   (c) Gateway (d) Field

Ans. :

285. (d)	286. (c)	287. (b)	288. (d)
289. (a)	290. (d)	291. (b)	292. (d)

293. Which type of computer network needs maximum networking cable:
   (a) Mesh Network (b) Ring Network
   (c) Star Network (d) Bus Network
294. What is Internet?
   (a) Network of networks
   (b) Network of International News
   (c) Networks of system
   (d) All the above
295. Electronic Document System is based on:
   (a) Optical Fiber System (b) Microwave System
   (c) Magnetic Tape (d) Optical Disc System
296. The first electronic document delivery system is:
   (a) UTLAS (b) OCLC
   (c) ADONIS (d) BLAISE
297. The first satellite communication project in India is:
   (a) APPLE (b) Telestar
   (c) ComSet (d) LV - 4
298. UNIVAC stands for:
   (a) Universal Automatic Analog Computer
   (b) Universal Automatic Calculation
   (c) Universal Analog Computer
   (d) Universal Automatic Computer
299. Questionnaire is a technique for collecting data used in System Analysis.
   (a) True (b) False

Ans. : 293. (c) 294. (a) 295. (d) 296. (c) 297. (a) 298. (d) 299. (a)

300. What does ADONIS stand for:

(a) Article Delivery Over National Information System

(b) Article Distribute Over Network Information System

(c) Article Delivery Over Network Information System

(d) Article Delivery On-line Information System

301. The first commercial computer name is:

(a) ABC (b) ABACUS

(c) UNIVAC (d) ENIVAC

302. Match the following:

(1) NICNET	(a) 1986
(2) ERNET	(b) 1988
(3) DELNET	(c) 1957
(4) CALIBNET	(d) 1977

Answers:

(a) 1 (d), 2 (a), 3 (b), 4 (a)

(b) 1 (a), 2 (c), 3 (b), 4 (d)

(c) 1 (a), 2 (d), 3 (c), 4 (b)

(d) 1 (c), 2 (d), 3 (a), 4 (b)

303. STAIRS stands for:

(a) Information Storage and Retrieval System

(b) Storage and Information Retrieval System

(c) Science and Technology Information Retrieval System

(d) Automatic Information Storage System

304. Concrete system is an example of visible boundaries:

(a) True (b) False

Ans. : 300. (c) 301. (c) 302. (a) 303. (b) 304. (a)

305. Hyper Text - Linkway was developed by IBM in the year 1989.
   (a) True (b) False

306. Page Maker is an example of:
   (a) Operating System
   (b) Electronic Spread Sheet
   (c) Application Software
   (d) DTP software

307. The name of first computerized database, developed by UNESCO is:
   (a) DARE (b) BIOSIS
   (c) TRUIP (d) EDUPLAN

308. What does VOIP stand for:
   (a) Visual Output Internet Protocol
   (b) Video Output - Input Protocol
   (c) Virus Over Internet Protocol
   (d) Virus Output Inter Protocol

309. Match the following:

(1) DOS	(a) 1969
(2) UNIX	(b) 1981
(3) Window- NT	(c) 1998
(4) CDS/ISIS	(d) 1985

   Answers:
   (a) 1 (a), 2 (b), 3 (c), 4 (d)
   (b) 1 (b), 2 (a), 3 (c), 4 (d)
   (c) 1 (b), 2 (d), 3 (a), 4 (c)
   (d) 1 (a), 2 (b), 3 (d), 4 (c)

Ans. : 305. (a) 306. (d) 307. (a) 308. (c) 309. (b)

310. DVD stands for:
   (a) Digital Video Drive
   (b) Digital Video Disc/ Digital Versatile Disc
   (c) Digital Video Diskette
   (d) Digital Visual Diagram

311. Co-axial is also known as:
   (a) Coox (b) Crux
   (c) Cruck (d) O-axial

312. Programming is a collection of instruction or commands:
   (a) True (b) False

313. A T & T stands for:
   (a) American Telecommunication Training
   (b) American Telephone and Telegram
   (c) American Telephone and Telegraph
   (d) American Telegraph Technology

314. Match the following:

(1) SIRNET	(a) 1969
(2) ARPANET	(b) 1981
(3) DELNET	(c) 1998

Answers:
   (a) 1 (b), 2 (a), 3 (c) (b) 1 (c), 2 (a), 3 (b)
   (c) 1 (a), 2 (c), 3 (b) (d) 1 (c), 2 (b), 3 (a)

315. PERT and CPM techniques are used in:
   (a) System development (b) Flowcharting
   (c) System Analysis (d) All the above

316. Telestar programme is launched by A T & T in July, 1962.
   (a) True (b) False

Ans. : 310. (b) 311. (a) 312. (a) 313. (c) 314. (b) 315. (c) 316. (a)

317. In CDS/ISIS help message can be visualized by pressing .... key.

(a) F1 (b) F2
(c) F4 (d) F6

318. CDS/ISIS - Windows version was came in:

(a) 1992 (b) 1993
(c) 1995 (d) 1996

319. A T & T is located at:

(a) UK (b) USA
(c) Italy (d) Canada

320. Under which organization Bell Laboratories functions:

(a) INTEL (b) IBM
(c) A T & T (d) InfoTech Consultant

321. Byte is a group of 8 bits.

(a) True (b) False

322. UNIX Operating System is developed by Ken Thompson and Bell Laboratories in the year 1969.

(a) True (b) False

323. The abbreviation TDCC stands for:

(a) Total Defence Communication Centre
(b) The Defence Development Computing Centre
(c) Training and Development Communication Channel Network
(d) Training and Development Computing Channel

324. Abbreviation CEMCA stands for:

(a) Commonwealth Educational Media for China
(b) Commonwealth Educational Media Centre for Asia
(c) Chemical Collection Media Centre
(d) None of the above

Ans. : 317. (a) 318. (d) 319. (b) 320. (c)
321. (a) 322. (a) 323. (c) 324. (b)

325. Which one is the full form of EMPC:
   (a) Electro Mechanical Personal Computer
   (b) Personal Computer - Electronic Machine
   (c) Electronic Media Programme Computing
   (d) Electronic Media Production Centre

326. OLS stands for:
   (a) Open Learning System (b) On-Line Service
   (c) Off-Line Service (d) On-Line Search

327. Abbreviation EDSAC stands for:
   (a) Electronic Display Storage Automatic Calculator
   (b) Electronic Delay Storage Automatic Calculator
   (c) Electronic Display Storage Automatic Computing
   (d) Electronic Delay Storage Automatic Communication

328. Universal Automatic Computer was developed by Mauchly and Eckert in 1951.
   (a) True (b) False

329. A database is nothing more than a computer based record-keeping system.
   (a) True (b) False

330. Personal Computer fall in the category of:
   (a) Mini Computer (b) Micro computer
   (c) Super Computer (d) Laptop Computer

331. What does EMCM stand for:
   (a) Electronic Mechanical Calculating Machine
   (b) Electronic Mechanical Computing Machine
   (c) Electro Mechanical Calculating Machine
   (d) Electro Mechanical Computing Machine

Ans. : 325. (d) 326. (a) 327. (b) 328. (a)
329. (a) 330. (b) 331. (c)

332. K I P S means:
    (a) Knowledge Information Providing System
    (b) Knowledge Information Processing System
    (c) Knowledge Information Processing Systems
    (d) None of the above
333. Digital Network Technology is developed in:
    (a) 1965 (b) 1970
    (c) 1975 (d) 1980
334. Which one is the full form of EPROM:
    (a) Erasable Programme Read Only Memory
    (b) Erasable Programmable Read Only Memory
    (c) Exchange Programmable Read Only Memory
    (d) Exchange Protocol Read Only Memory
335. What is BIOSIS?
    (a) Network (b) Software
    (c) Database (d) Computer Device
336. ICRISAT is located at:
    (a) Ahmedabad (b) Hyderabad
    (c) Haryana (d) Allahabad
337. Hewlett Packard's version of UNIX is known as HP-UX.
    (a) Tue (b) False
338. MATHSCI and GEOREF are:
    (a) Software (b) Network
    (c) Programming language (d) Database
339. TYMNET, TELENET, and ERNET are an example of:
    (a) Communication Network (b) Database
    (c) System Software (d) Local Area Network

Ans. :	332. (c)	333. (d)	334. (b)	335. (c)
	336. (b)	337. (a)	338. (d)	339. (a)

340. What is NAN:
    (a) New York Network
    (b) Neighborhood Area Network
    (c) North Area Network
    (d) None of these
341. Advantages of CD-ROM are:
    (a) Ease to use (b) Speedy retrieval
    (c) High storage capacity (d) All the above
342. Multimedia Information System includes many different types of media such as text, record-based data, numeric data, graphics, image, voice and video.
    (a) True (b) False
343. OS-2 (operating system) is designed by:
    (a) E T & T (b) A T & T
    (c) IBM
    (d) Microsoft Cooperation Ltd.
344. The facility available in Internet is:
    (a) E-Commerce (b) Distance learning
    (c) Direct communication (d) All the above
345. Abbreviation DOI stands for:
    (a) Digital Object Identifier
    (b) Direct Input & Output
    (c) Documentation and Information
    (d) Dot per Inch
346. What does ISDN stand for:
    (a) Indian Standards for Digital Network
    (b) Input Services for Digital Network
    (c) Integrated Services Digital Network
    (d) None of the above

Ans. : 340. (b) 341. (d) 342. (a) 343. (c)
344. (d) 345. (a) 346. (c)

347. 'Hyper Text means non-sequential writing' said by:
   (a) V. Bush (b) T. H. Nelson
   (c) D. J. Faskett (d) Prof. Yashpal
348. National Centre for Supercomputing is also known as:
   (a) NCSA (b) NACSA
   (c) NACSUA (d) NCSAP
349. Non-bibliographic databases contain:
   (a) Textual data (b) Visual data
   (c) Numeric data (d) Both 'A' and 'B'
350 The advantages of Hyper Media are:
   (a) Main output in visual form
   (b) Optimum freedom in visual form
   (c) Databases can be updated at any time
   (d) All of the above
351 In the content of computer, what is 'Mouse'?
   (a) Software (b) Hardware
   (c) Language (d) Name of computer
352. Match the following:

(1) Bit	(a) 1969
(2) Byte	(b) 1981
(3) Nibble	(c) 1998

   Answers:
   (a) 1 (a), 2 (b), 3 (c) (b) 1 (c), 2 (a), 3 (b)
   (c) 1 (a), 2 (c), 3 (b) (d) 1 (b), 2 (a), 3 (c)
353. Abbreviation CRDB stands for:
   (a) Computer Readable Data Base
   (b) Computer Readable Data Bank
   (c) Co-Readable Book Data Base
   (d) C-Book Data Base

Ans. : 347. (b) 348. (a) 349. (c) 350. (d)
351. (b) 352. (c) 353. (a)

354. INFLIBNET is an example of:
   (a) LAN (b) MAN
   (c) WAN (d) Global Network

355. Logical Operator AND, OR and NOT were devised by:
   (a) Charles Babbage (b) George Boole
   (c) Vannever Bush (d) Herman Hollerith

356. DELNET was setup at New Delhi in 1992 under:
   (a) Library Registration Act, 1992
   (b) Library Registration Act, 1991
   (c) Societies Registration Act, 1980
   (d) Societies Registration Act, 1992

357. Which service is provided by DELNET:
   (a) Inter library lone online services
   (b) Internet and e-mail services
   (c) Data thesis & dissertation services
   (d) All the above

358. The code, used for cataloguing by DELNET is:
   (a) CCC (b) AACR - II
   (c) BSO (d) A A Code

359. The memory capacity of a computer measured in:
   (a) Hertz (b) Bytes
   (c) KBPS (d) Chips

360. Which of the following is not a microform:
   (a) Aperture card (b) Microform
   (c) Microfiche (d) Micro computer

361. On-line information system comes under the category of:
   (a) Database generator (b) Database vendor
   (c) Database producer (d) Database consultant

Ans. : 354. (c) 355. (b) 356. (c) 357. (d) 358. (b) 359. (c) 360. (d) 361. (b)

362. LibSys is:
    (a) An application software (b) A library software
    (c) Both 'A' and 'B' (d) None of these
363. Mark the odd one:
    (a) Ventura (b) MS - Word
    (c) Page Maker (d) Lotos
364. In the context of telecommunication, abbreviation WILL stand for:
    (a) Wireless Language Local Loop
    (b) Wireless in Local Loop
    (c) Wireless & Infrared Local Loop
    (d) Wipro Library Limited
365. Mark the odd one:
    (a) Micro computer, Macro computer, PC-AT, PC-XT
    (b) Micro computer, Macro computer, PC-XT, PC-AT
    (c) PC-AT, PC-XT, Super computer
    (d) PC-XT, PC-AT, Micro computer
366. Wireless in Local Loop (WILL) techniques is success in:
    (a) Limited area (b) Local area
    (c) Wide area (d) All of the above
367. Who is the present director of INFLIBNET:
    (a) DR. A. P. Gakhar (b) Dr. T. A. V. Murthy
    (c) Dr. Jagdish Arora (d) Pandey S. K. Sharma
368. Which one is the main function of INFLIBNET:
    (a) Library Networking (b) Inter library loan
    (c) Software development (d) All the above
369. Which one of the following networks does not have to own tele-communication infrastructure:
    (a) INIS (b) NICNET
    (c) ERNET (d) EURONET

Ans. : 362. (c) 363. (d) 364. (b) 365. (b) 366. (a) 367. (c) 368. (a) 369. (c)

370. Which one of the following is a part of the MARC record structure:

(a) Directory (b) Leader

(c) Cheek Digit (d) Both (a) and (b)

371. The device that converts digital to analog and analog to digital signals is known as Modem.

(a) True (b) False

372. Boolean searching:

(a) Based on Post Coordinate indexing

(b) Combines search statements using 'AND', 'OR' and 'NOT'

(c) Both (a) and (b)

(d) Neither (a) and (b)

373. Which of the following network is not involved in content provision:

(a) INIS (b) OCLC

(c) I-NET (d) MEDLARS

374. Which of the following network is not primarily for academic purpose:

(a) JANET (b) NICNET

(c) INFLIBNET (d) ERNET

375. The useful input device is:

(a) Keyboard (b) CD-ROMs

(c) Light Pens (d) All the above

376. Which language is suitable for scientific computers :

(a) PL-1 (b) Algol

(c) PASCAL (d) FORTRAN

Ans. : 370. (d) 371. (a) 372. (c) 373. (d) 374. (b) 375. (d) 376. (a)

377. CD-ROM is a powerful tool for storage and retrieval of large amounts of data.
    (a) True (b) False

378. Mark the odd one (clue: Resource Sharing):
    (a) RLIN (b) BIOSIS
    (c) OCLC (d) INFLIBNET

379. ————————— has made library network very convenient:
    (a) Computer
    (b) Star Network
    (c) INFLIBNET
    (d) Information Technology

380. Which of the following is not a spreadsheet software:
    (a) Excel (b) Lotus 1 2 3
    (c) Lucid-3D (d) dBase

381. Which option is given in WordStar for opening a file:
    (a) A (b) D
    (c) F (d) H

382. The second generation computer used transistor for their CPU:
    (a) True (b) False

383. Who is the Present director of DELNET:
    (a) Prof. Yashpal (b) V. K. Shinha
    (c) Dr. H. K .Kaul (d) Krishan Kumar

384. 'DELMARC' and 'DELPLUS' software packages are presented by:
    (a) NICNET (b) DELNET
    (c) ADINET (d) UUNET

Ans. :	377. (a)	378. (b)	379. (d)	380. (d)
	381. (b)	382. (a)	383. (c)	384. (b)

385. The abbreviation CLIC stands for:
   (a) Computerized Library Centre
   (b) Compute Library and Information Centre
   (c) Computerized Library and Information Centre
   (d) None of these

386. ASCII is a 7 bits binary code used to encode character on a computer.
   (a) True (b) False

387. Modern Computer was developed by Charles Babbage.
   (a) True (b) False

388. What does AARNET stand for:
   (a) An Academic Research Network
   (b) Advanced Academic Research Network
   (c) Austria Academic Research Network
   (d) Australian Academic Research Network

389. Which one is the following is known as the Academic Research Network in the Netherland:
   (a) JANET (b) AARNET
   (c) SURFNET (d) UTLAS

390. Software Technology Parks in India (STPI) is a society set up by Ministry of Information Technology, Govt. of India in the year 1991.
   (a) True (b) False

391. Abbreviation WLAN stands for:
   (a) Wireless in Local Loop Area Network
   (b) Wireless Local Area Network
   (c) Wide-Local Area Network
   (d) None of the above

Ans. : 385. (c) 386. (a) 387. (a) 388. (d)
389. (c) 390. (a) 391. (b)

392. XML stands for:
   (a) eXtensive Memory Language
   (b) Xtech Markup Language
   (c) eXtensive Markup Language
   (d) All the above
393. The full form of PSTN is:
   (a) Public Switched Transmission Network
   (b) Pre-switched Transmission Network
   (c) Public Service Transmission Network
   (d) Public Switched Telephone Network
394. What does SGML stand for:
   (a) Standard Generalized Markup Language
   (b) Serial Generalized Markup Language
   (c) System Generalized Markup Language
   (d) All the above
395. The Government of India passed cyber laws as in the parliament in the year 2000.
   (a) True (b) False
396. In which country, BITNET is introduced:
   (a) China (b) UK
   (c) USA (d) Japan
397. I-NET is first PSPDN (Pocket Switching Public Data Network) to provide communication units across major metropolis of India.
   (a) True (b) False
398. Abbreviation VPN stands for:
   (a) Visual Picture Network
   (b) Video Programme Network
   (c) Virtual Private Network
   (d) None of the above

Ans. : 392. (c) 393. (d) 394. (a) 395. (a) 396. (c) 397. (a) 398. (c)

399. Bar Code technology is a most accurate and least expensive to identify item/document and get data into the computer.

(a) True (b) False

400. POPLINE is an online service provided by:

(a) INIS (b) MEDLARS

(c) INSPEC (d) WHO

401. POPLINE is an online service provided by:

(a) BARC (b) INIS

(c) INSPEC (d) AGRIS

402. 'Ocean Line' database created by:

(a) Oceanography Institute of India, New Delhi

(b) Institute of Oceanography & Sea Culture, Pune

(c) National Institute of Oceanography

(d) None of the above

403. An online information system comes under the category of:

(a) Database Generator (b) Database Vendor

(c) Database Producer (d) Database Consultant

404. RFID stands for:

(a) Reference, Information & Documentation

(b) Reference Frequency IDentification

(c) Radio Frequency Documentation

(d) Radio Frequency Identification

405. RFID is a combination of radio-frequency-based technology and microchip technology.

(a) True (b) False

Ans. : 399. (a) 400. (b) 401. (c) 402. (c)
403. (b) 404. (d) 405. (a)

406. A digital library is 'a managed collection of information, with associated services, where the information is stored in digital formats and accessible over a network'.

(a) True (b) False

Ans. : 406. (a)

3

Information Institutions, Systems, Products and Services

1. What does TLD stand for:
   (a) Telecommunication and Documentation
   (b) Training in Librarianship and Documentation
   (c) Training in Documentation for Librarianship
   (d) Total Library Development Programme
2. Smith Sorian Institute of Science Information is an example of:
   (a) Information Centre (b) Data Centre
   (c) Referral Centre (d) Clearing House
3. Which one is the full form of NICRYS:
   (a) NISSAT Centre on Crystallography
   (b) National Information Centre on Crystallography
   (c) National Information Centre on Chemical Research
   (d) None of the above

Ans. : 1. (b) 2. (d) 3. (b)

4. Under which organization Institute of Himalayan Bio-Technology functions:
   (a) CSIR (b) ICSSR
   (c) INSDOC (d) DRTC
5. IHBT is located at:
   (a) Mysore (b) Kolkata
   (c) Bangalore (d) Palampur
6. Indian Institute of Chemical Biology is located at:
   (a) Pune (b) New Delhi
   (c) Kolkata (d) Hyderabad
7. The abbreviation NAL stands for:
   (a) NASSDOC Library
   (b) National Aerospace Laboratory
   (c) NISSAT Aerospace Laboratories
   (d) National Library, Kolkata
8. National Aerospace Laboratory is initiated by:
   (a) NISCAIR (b) DRDO
   (c) NISSAT (d) CSIR
9. COSIST Programme is related to UGC, India.
   (a) True (b) False
10. National Aerospace Laboratory is located at:
    (a) Pune (b) Patna
    (c) Indore (d) NOIDA
11. What does UNIDO stand for:
    (a) UNESCO - Indian Digital On-line Project
    (b) UNESCO - NISCAIR Project
    (c) UNESCO - INIS Digital Project
    (d) United Nations Industrial Development Organization

Ans. : 4. (a) 5. (c) 6. (c) 7. (b)
8. (d) 9. (a) 10. (a) 11. (d)

12. NIO is initiated by:
    (a) ICAR (b) CSIR
    (c) DRDO (d) NISSAT
13. National Institute of Oceanography is located at:
    (a) Jadugoda Mines (b) Chandigarh
    (c) Bargarh (d) Goa
14. SERC stands for:
    (a) Structural Engineering Research Centre
    (b) Structural Engineering Reference Centre
    (c) Structural Engineering Referral Centre
    (d) Scientific and Electronic Retrieval Centre
15. SERC laboratory is initiated by CSIR in the year:
    (a) 1961 (b) 1963
    (c) 1966 (d) 1969
16. Structural Engineering Research Centre is located at:
    (a) New Delhi (b) Kolkata
    (c) Bombay (d) Chennai
17. MEDLARS is started by:
    (a) Indian Medical Association
    (b) National Library of Medicine, USA
    (c) American Library Association
    (d) Indian Council of Medical Research

Ans. : 12. (b) 13. (d) 14. (a) 15. (c) 16. (d) 17. (b)

18. Match the following:

(1) INSDOC	(a) SIET
(2) NASSDOC	(b) CSIR
(3) SENDOC	(c) DRDO
(4) DESIDOC	(d) ICSSR

Answers:

(a) 1 (b), 2 (d), 3 (a), 4 (c)
(b) 1 (b), 2 (d), 3 (c), 4 (a)
(c) 1 (b), 2 (a), 3 (d), 4 (c)
(d) 1 (d), 2 (b), 3 (a), 4 (c)

19. MEDLARS is a computerized bibliographical retrieval system.
(a) True (b) False

20. 'National Information System for Science & Technology' programme is initiated in:
(a) 1960 (b) 1967
(c) 1970 (d) 1977

21. I I P stands for:
(a) Indian Institute of Petroleum
(b) Petroleum Information Institute
(c) Institute of Petroleum Information
(d) Indian Patent Institute

22. Indian Institute of Petroleum is working under:
(a) DRDO (b) SIET
(c) SENDOC (d) CSIR

23. RRL stands for:
(a) Regional Research Library
(b) Regional Research Laboratory
(c) Research Report Laboratory
(d) Regional Report Library

Ans. : 18. (a) 19. (a) 20. (c) 21. (a)
22. (d) 23. (b)

24. BARC is located at:
   (a) Mumbai (b) Bargarh
   (c) Mangalore (d) Ahmedabad

25. Match the following:
   (1) CARIS (a) Social Science
   (2) DARE (b) Medical Science
   (3) DELMS (c) Defence Science
   (4) MEDLARS (d) Agriculture

   Answers:
   (a) 1 (a), 2 (c), 3 (d), 4 (b)
   (b) 1 (b), 2 (a), 3 (c), 4 (d)
   (c) 1 (d), 2 (a), 3 (c), 4 (b)
   (d) 1 (c), 2 (d), 3 (b), 4 (a)

26. Abbreviation BARC stands for:
   (a) Bhabha Atomic Research Committee
   (b) Bhabha Atomic Referral Centre
   (c) Bhattacharya Atomic Research Centre
   (d) Bhabha Atomic Research Centre

27. What does IAEA stand for:
   (a) Indian Atomic Energy Agency
   (b) International Atomic Energy Agency
   (c) Indian Aerospace Agency
   (d) International Aerospace Agency

28. INIS is initiated by IAEA in the year:
   (a) April, 1975 (b) April, 1974
   (c) April, 1970 (d) April, 1968

29. The headquarter of INIS is located at:
   (a) New York (b) The Huge
   (c) Vienna (Austria) (d) Delft

Ans. : 24. (a) 25. (c) 26. (d) 27. (b) 28. (c) 29. (c)

30. INIS stands for:
    (a) International Nuclear Information System
    (b) International Network Information System
    (c) Indian Nuclear Information System
    (d) Information Network Services
31. Which one is the full form of the DRDO:
    (a) Defence Research & Developing Organisation
    (b) Defence Research & Development Organisation
    (c) Documentation Research Development Organisation
    (d) None of the above
32. Match the following:

(1) PADIS	(a) Pakistan
(2) CNRS	(b) France
(3) VINITI	(c) Ethopia
(4) PASTIC	(d) Russian

    Answers:
    (a) 1 (a), 2 (b), 3 (d), 4 (c)
    (b) 1 (a), 2 (c), 3 (d), 4 (b)
    (c) 1 (c), 2 (b), 3 (d), 4 (a)
    (d) 1 (b), 2 (c), 3 (d), 4 (a)
33. Indian Reniable Energy Development Agency is situated at:
    (a) New Delhi (b) Mumbai
    (c) Kolkata (d) Kanpur
34. The full form of TRUIP is:
    (a) Training and Research Unit in PADIS
    (b) Training Units in research
    (c) PADIS Units for Training & Research
    (d) Teaching Research Units in Science & Technology Policies

---

Ans. : 30. (a) 31. (b) 32. (c) 33. (a) 34. (d)

35. CISTI is located at:
    (a) China (b) Canada
    (c) India (d) USA
36. APINESS programme is launched by UNESCO at Paris in 1974.
    (a) True (b) False
37. The another name of UNISIST is:
    (a) World Science Information System
    (b) Information System for Science & Technology
    (c) United Nations information System
    (d) UNESCO Science Project
38. 'UNISIST - Study report on the feasibility of a world Science Information System' was published in the year:
    (a) 1950 (b) 1960
    (c) 1967 (d) 1970
39. UNISIST Newsletters was first published in:
    (a) 1970 (b) 1972
    (c) 1976 (d) 1979
40. The year of establishment of DRDO is:
    (a) 1958 (b) 1968
    (c) 1972 (d) 1978
41. Match the following:
    (1) INIS (a) FAO-UNO
    (2) AGRIS (b) UNESCO-ICSU
    (3) NATIS (c) IAEA
    (4) UNISIST (d) UNESCO

    Answers:
    (a) 1 (b), 2 (a), 3 (c), 4 (d)
    (b) 1 (b), 2 (a), 3 (d), 4 (b)
    (c) 1 (c), 2 (a), 3 (d), 4 (b)
    (d) 1 (c), 2 (a), 3 (d), 4 (b)

Ans. : 35. (b) 36. (a) 37. (a) 38. (d)
39. (b) 40. (a) 41. (c)

42. UNISIST stands for:
    (a) UNESCO Information System in Science & Technology
    (b) UNESCO information Service for Scientific Technique
    (c) United Nations information System in Science & Technology
    (d) United Nations information System
43. Under which organization DESIDOC functions:
    (a) DELMS (b) DRDO
    (c) BARC (d) NASA
44. The year of establishment of CSIR is:
    (a) 1942 (b) 1944
    (c) 1948 (d) 1949
45. The Headquarter of CSIR is located at:
    (a) New Delhi (b) NOIDA
    (c) Hyderabad (d) Ghaziabad
46. What does SIET stand for:
    (a) Small Enterprises
    (b) Small Industries Enterprises
    (c) Small Industries Extension Training
    (d) Small Industries Extension Programme
47. The Sponsoring body of SENDOC is:
    (a) CSIR (b) ICSSR
    (c) NCL (d) SIET
48. NISSAT is the focal point in India for the UNESCO/UNISIST programme.
    (a) True (b) False

Ans. : 42. (c) 43. (b) 44. (a) 45. (a)
46. (c) 47. (d) 48. (a)

49. AIIMS is located at:

(a) Varanasi (b) New Delhi
(c) Keonjhar (d) Faridabad

50. Abbreviation AIIMS stands for:

(a) All India Institute of Medical Standards
(b) All India Institute of Management Sciences
(c) All India Institute of Medical Sciences
(d) All India Institute of Micro Sciences

51. Abbreviation ICAR stands for:

(a) Indian Council of Agricultural Research
(b) Indian Centre for Agricultural Research
(c) Indian Council for Agriculture
(d) None of the above

52. The year of establishment of ICAR is:

(a) 1911 (b) 1913
(c) 1929 (d) 1942

53. The headquarter of ICAR at Pusa was shifted to New Delhi in:

(a) 1929 (b) 1913
(c) 1919 (d) 1942

54. In India the major internet service provider is:

(a) NIC (b) DOE
(c) CMC (d) VSNL

55. The first headquarter of ICAR was situated at:

(a) New Delhi (b) Mumbai
(c) Punjab (d) Pusa

Ans. : 49. (b) 50. (c) 51. (a) 52. (b)
53. (a) 54. (d) 55. (d)

56. TFIR stands for:
    (a) Tata Fundamental and Industrial Research
    (b) Total Fundamental Information Research
    (c) Tata Fundamental and Industrial Report
    (d) Tata Food Information Centre

57. Abbreviation ISRO stands for:
    (a) Indian Social Research Organization
    (b) Indian Science Research Organization
    (c) Indian Space Research Organization
    (d) Indo-China Space Research Organization

58. National Contact Point (NCP) for APINESS in India is NASSDOC.
    (a) True (b) False

59. Match the following:

(1) SARC	(a) Mumbai
(2) ISRO	(b) Chennai
(3) SERC	(c) Shri Harikota
(4) BARC	(d) Ahmedabad

Answers:
    (a) 1 (a), 2 (d), 3 (c), 4 (b)
    (b) 1 (c), 2 (d), 3 (b), 4 (a)
    (c) 1 (d), 2 (c), 3 (b), 4 (a)
    (d) 1 (b), 2 (a), 3 (c), 4 (d)

60. The year of establishment of Vikram Sarabhai Space Centre is:
    (a) 1942 (b) 1952
    (c) 1962 (d) 1972

Ans. : 56. (a) 57. (c) 58. (a) 59. (b) 60. (d)

61. Vikram Sarabhai Space Centre is located at:
    (a) Trivandrum (b) Shri Harikota
    (c) Sambhalpur (d) Ahmedabad
62. ASCI stands for:
    (a) Advertisement Standard Council of INDO-China
    (b) Advertisement Standard Council of India
    (c) American Standard Council for Research
    (d) An American Standard Council
63. FID/CR project was set up in the year:
    (a) 1962 (b) 1968
    (c) 1972 (d) 1978
64. Who is the publisher of 'Index Medicus':
    (a) MEDLARS (b) NLM
    (c) IMA (d) CITTU
65. 'Index Medicus' was first published in:
    (a) 1974 (b) 1973
    (c) 1969 (d) 1976
66. Abridge edition of Index Medicus (AIM) was first published in the year:
    (a) 1964 (b) 1970
    (c) 1974 (d) 1976
67. BSI is a national standard body of:
    (a) India (b) Bangladesh
    (c) United Kingdom (d) USA
68. The name of national standard body of USA is:
    (a) ANSI (b) ASNI
    (c) ANTI (d) ANSTI

Ans. :

61. (a)	62. (b)	63. (c)	64. (a)
65. (d)	66. (b)	67. (c)	68. (a)

69. BIS stands for:
    (a) British Standard Institute
    (b) British Information Service
    (c) Bachelor of Information Science
    (d) Bureau of Indian Standards

70. BIS is the national standard body of:
    (a) Nepal (b) India
    (c) UK (d) Indonesia

71. What was the name of BSI earlier?
    (a) National Standard Institute
    (b) Bureau of Indian Information Centers
    (c) Indian Standard Institute
    (d) Indian Standard Bureau

72. What does BSI stand for:
    (a) British Standard Institute
    (b) Bureau of Indian Standards
    (c) Bureau of British Standards
    (d) None of the above

73. The abbreviation ANSI stands for:
    (a) National Standard Institute, America
    (b) American National Standards Institute
    (c) National Standard Institute of America
    (d) National Standard Institute of Austria

Ans. : 69. (d) 70. (b) 71. (c) 72. (a)
73. (b)

74. Match the following:

(1) IARE	(a) Thermophysical properties
(2) IISC	(b) Petroleum
(3) IIP	(c) Documentation
(4) DRTC	(d) Agriculture

Answers:

(a) 1 (d), 2 (c), 3 (b), 4 (a)
(b) 1 (d), 2 (a), 3 (c), 4 (b)
(c) 1 (d), 2 (c), 3 (a), 4 (b)
(d) 1 (d), 2 (a), 3 (b), 4 (c)

75. Which one is the full form of ISO:
(a) International Organization for Standards
(b) International Standards Organization
(c) International Organization for Standardization
(d) International Standards Institute

76. The Present name of ISO is:
(a) ISO/TC-46 (b) ISO-46
(c) ISO/TCP/I46 (d) ISO-TCP

77. National Council of Scientific Research is situated at:
(a) Germany (b) Russia
(c) France (d) Canada

78. European Translation Centre is situated at:
(a) New York (b) Delft, Nederland
(c) Paris (d) Net west

79. CNRS is also known as:
(a) Council of National Scientific Research
(b) National Council of Scientific Research
(c) National Council of Scientific Research
(d) Council of National Science Research

Ans. : 74. (d) 75. (c) 76. (a) 77. (c) 78. (b) 79. (c)

80. The abbreviation ISI stands for:
    (a) Institute of Scientific information
    (b) Indian Standards Institute
    (c) Indian Information Society
    (d) None of the above
81. Institute of Scientific Information (ISI) is located at:
    (a) China (b) India
    (c) Philadelphia (d) London
82. Under which organization NACID functions:
    (a) UNESCO (b) UNISIST
    (c) NISCAIR (d) NISSAT
83. INPAT is created by:
    (a) INPADOC (b) NASSDOC
    (c) INSDOC (d) NISSAT
84. What does INPAT stands for:
    (a) Indian Patent
    (b) International Patent
    (c) Indian Patent Association
    (d) International Patent Association
85. NACID stands for:
    (a) NASSDOC Centre for International Data
    (b) NISSAT Access Centre to International Data
    (c) National Centre for Information and Documentation
    (d) None of these

Ans. : 80. (a) 81. (c) 82. (d) 83. (c) 84. (a) 85. (a)

86. Match the following:

(1) BIS	(a) UK
(2) DIN	(b) Germany
(3) BSI	(c) India
(4) ANSI	(d) USA

Answers:

(a) 1 (a), 2 (b), 3 (c), 4 (d)
(b) 1 (a), 2 (d), 3 (c), 4 (b)
(c) 1 (c), 2 (b), 3 (a), 4 (d)
(d) 1 (c), 2 (d), 3 (b), 4 (a)

87. What is BLDSC:
(a) Document Supply Centre (b) Translation Centre
(c) Data Centre (d) Referral Centre

88. What is the name of ISO earlier?
(a) International Organisation for Standards
(b) International Standards Organisation
(c) International Standard Association
(d) International Association for Standardization

89. BLDSC is set up by:
(a) BLAISE (b) British Library (UK)
(c) JANET (d) ARPANET

90. The full form of BLDSC is:
(a) British Library Document Supply Centre
(b) Bibliography and Document Supply Centre
(c) British Document Supply Centre
(d) British Library Document Supply Centre- Network

Ans. : 86. (c) 87. (a) 88. (c) 89. (b) 90. (a)

91. The national standard body of Germany is:
    (a) Distance Information Network
    (b) Deutsches institute of Nursing
    (c) Digital Information Standards Institute
    (d) Document Standards Institute
92. BLLP means:
    (a) British Project for London Libraries
    (b) British Library Lending Project
    (c) British Library Lending Provision
    (d) Library Lending Provision for British Library
93. DDC is an example of:
    (a) Data Centre
    (b) Documentation Centre
    (c) Information Analysis Centre
    (d) Referral Centre
94. What does ADONIS stand for:
    (a) Article Delivery Over Network Information Service
    (b) Article Delivery On-line Information System
    (c) Article Delivery Over Network Information System
    (d) Article Delivery On-line Information Service
95. Abbreviation SAARC stands for:
    (a) South Asian Association for Referral Centre
    (b) South Asian Association for Regional Cooperation
    (c) South Asian Association for Research Centre
    (d) None of the above

Ans. : 91. (b) 92. (c) 93. (d) 94. (c) 95. (b)

96. CASEARCH is the short name of:
    (a) Chemical search
    (b) Current Abstract Search
    (c) Chemical Abstract Search
    (d) Chemical AVIS Search
97. First modern house journal was published by J M Peterson, USA in 1887.
    (a) True (b) False
98. Defence Documentation Centre is located at:
    (a) India (b) UK
    (c) USA (d) Shri Lanka
99. What is UNEP:
    (a) IAC
    (b) Documentation Centre
    (c) Referral Centre
    (d) Patent Information System
100. Which one is the full form of CMTRI:
    (a) Centre for Marine Technique Research Institute
    (b) Centre for Machine Tools Research Institute
    (c) Computing Tools Research Institute
    (d) None of the above
101. The name of trade directory of India is:
    (a) Indian Books in Print
    (b) Trade Directory of India
    (c) AVIS Trade Directory of India
    (d) Kotharies Industrial Directory of India

Ans. : 96. (c) 97. (a) 98. (c) 99. (c) 100. (b) 101. (d)

102. Match the following:

(1) ICMR	(a) Medical Information
(2) Predicast (USA)	(b) Oceanography
(3) NCI	(c) Economic Information
(4) NIO	(d) Chemical Subject

Answers:

(a) 1 (a), 2 (d), 3 (b), 4 (c)
(b) 1 (a), 2 (c), 3 (d), 4 (b)
(c) 1 (a), 2 (b), 3 (d), 4 (c)
(d) 1 (a), 2 (c), 3 (b), 4 (d)

103. SAIL is located at:

(a) Lucknow (b) Jabalpur
(c) Kanpur (d) Ranchi

104. STAR stands for:

(a) Science and Technology Reference Service
(b) Science and Technology Report
(c) Science Information System
(d) Scientific and Technical Aerospace Report

105. What does UNEP stand for:

(a) United Nations Environmental Programme
(b) UNESCO Educational Programme
(c) UNISIST Network
(d) UNO Programmes for Higher Education

106. CODATA was initiated by ICSU in the year 1966.

(a) True (b) False

107. Dewent is located at:

(a) Delft (b) Paris
(c) London (d) New York

Ans. : 102. (b) 103. (d) 104. (d) 105. (a) 106. (a) 107. (c)

108. The abbreviation INODC stands for:
    (a) Indian National Oceanic Data Centre
    (b) Indian National Oceanography Data Centre
    (c) International Oceanography Data Centre
    (d) Indian Oceanic Data Centre

109. INODC is an example of:
    (a) Data Centre (b) Referral Centre
    (c) IAC (d) Clearing House

110. Abbreviation NATIS stands for:
    (a) National Information Service
    (b) National Information System
    (c) National Information Systems and Services
    (d) National Technical Information Service

111. 'Commission on Science and Technology in Development Countries' (COSTED) is a programme of ICSU, started in 1966.
    (a) True (b) False

112. SAIL stands for:
    (a) Steel Authority of Industrial Limited
    (b) Steel Authority of India Limited
    (c) South Asian On-line Network
    (d) None of the above

113. DGMS means:
    (a) Defence General Medical Science
    (b) DESIDOC Digital Media Centre
    (c) Directered and General of Medical Specialist
    (d) DESIDOC General, Media Services

Ans. : 108. (a) 109. (b) 110. (a) 111. (a) 112. (b) 113. (c)

114. Patent Atorny is:
   (a) Patent Specialist
   (b) Legal Advises of Patent
   (c) Standard
   (d) Directory
115. The Headquarter of GAIL is situated at:
   (a) New Delhi (b) Jadugoda Mines
   (c) Kanpur (d) Karnataka
116. INFOTEL is initiated by:
   (a) NIC (b) Microsoft
   (c) Informatics India Limited
   (d) Softlink
117. IISC stands for:
   (a) Indian Science Institute
   (b) Institute of Information Science
   (c) Indian Institute of Scientific Information
   (d) Indian Institute of Science
118. POPINS is an information system for:
   (a) Information Policy (b) Population
   (c) Budget (d) Research
119. Match the following:

(1) DTIC	(a) UK
(2) DRIC	(b) USA
(3) SSRC	(c) India
(4) IISC	(d) Australia

   Answers:
   (a) 1 (a), 2 (b), 3 (b), 4 (c)
   (b) 1 (b), 2 (a), 3 (b), 4 (c)
   (c) 1 (a), 2 (b), 3 (d), 4 (c)
   (d) 1 (b), 2 (d), 3 (a), 4 (c)

Ans. : 114. (b) 115. (a) 116. (c) 117. (d) 118. (b) 119. (b)

120. What does POPINS stand for:
    (a) Population Information System
    (b) Project Information System
    (c) Pollution Information System
    (d) None of the above
121. IRISS is located at:
    (a) France (b) USA
    (c) UK (d) Ethiopia
122. GAIL stands for:
    (a) Gas Authority of India Limited
    (b) Glass Authority of India Limited
    (c) Both (a) and (b)
    (d) None of the above
123. ICSSRDC is situated at:
    (a) BKM, Varanasi (b) BHU, Varanasi
    (c) JNU, New Delhi (d) AMU, Aligarh
124. DTIC is an example of:
    (a) Data Centre (b) Information Centre
    (c) Clearing House (d) IAC
125. IRISS stands for:
    (a) Indian Research in Social Science
    (b) Information Retrieval System and Services
    (c) Information Retrieval in Social Sciences
    (d) Institute for Research in Social Sciences
126. DRIC is an example of:
    (a) Referral Centre
    (b) Data Centre
    (c) Information Centre
    (d) Information Analysis Centre

Ans. : 120. (a) 121. (c) 122. (a) 123. (c)
124. (b) 125. (d) 126. (c)

127. SSRC is situated at:
    (a) Brazil (b) France
    (c) Canada (d) USA
128. Indian Institute of Science (IISC) is located at:
    (a) Ahmedabad
    (b) Bengaluru
    (c) Hyderabad
    (d) Faridabad
129. Abbreviation DRIC stands for:
    (a) Defence Research Information Centre
    (b) DRDO Information Centre
    (c) DESIDOC Research & Information Centre
    (d) None of the above
130. DTIC stands for:
    (a) Defence Topic and information Communication
    (b) Defence Technical Information Centre
    (c) DESIDOC Technical Information Centre
    (d) DELMS Technique and Services
131. Information Filter is an essential mediator between information sources and their users.
    (a) True (b) False
132. What is ICA:
    (a) Information Analysis Centre
    (b) Information Council for Library Automation
    (c) International Council on Archives
    (d) Indian Computing Agency

Ans. : 127. (d) 128. (b) 129. (a) 130. (b) 131. (a) 132. (c)

133. Match the following:

(1) INSDOC	(a) 1952
(2) NASSDOC	(b) 1958
(3) SENDOC	(c) 1970
(4) DESIDOC	(d) 1971

Answers:

(a) 1 (a), 2 (b), 3 (c), 4 (d)

(b) 1 (a), 2 (c), 3 (d), 4 (b)

(c) 1 (a), 2 (c), 3 (b), 4 (d)

(d) 1 (a), 2 (d), 3 (c), 4 (b)

134. ISORID project was started by:

(a) NISCAIR (b) NISSAT

(c) IFLA (d) FID

135. NASA is located at:

(a) Chicago (b) Paris

(c) USA (d) Ahmedabad

136. Abbreviation ICSU stands for:

(a) International Council of Scientific Unions

(b) Indian Council of Scientific Unions

(c) Information Centre on Scientific Units

(d) Council of Science & Technology Units

137. The term 'Information Retrieval' was first used by:

(a) Mikhailav and Gilyarevaski

(b) S. C. Bradford

(c) F. W. Lancaster

(d) Colvin Moores

Ans. : 133. (b) 134. (d) 135. (c) 136. (a) 137. (d)

138. What does ILRC stand for:
   (a) Inter Library Referral Centre
   (b) Inter Library Resource Centre
   (c) Indian Library Resources Centre
   (d) None of the above

139. IDRC stands for:
   (a) International Development Research Centre
   (b) Indian Documentation & Research Centre
   (c) INSDOC Data Retrieval Centre
   (d) INSDOC Data Research Centre

140. Inter Library Resource Centre is set up by :
   (a) NISCAIR (b) DESIDOC
   (c) SENDOC (d) NASSDOC

141. The abbreviation NASA stands for:
   (a) National Aerospace Agency
   (b) National Atomic and Space Agency
   (c) National Aeronautics and Space Administration
   (d) National Aeronautics Atomic Space Agency

142. Match the following:

(1) MEDLARS	(a) Netherlands
(2) AGRIS	(b) Austria
(3) INIS	(c) USA
(4) FID	(d) Rome

Answers:
   (a) 1 (a), 2 (d), 3 (c), 4 (b)
   (b) 1 (c), 2 (d), 3 (b), 4 (d)
   (c) 1 (b), 2 (a), 3 (c), 4 (a)
   (d) 1 (c), 2 (a), 3 (b), 4 (d)

Ans. : 138. (b) 139. (a) 140. (d) 141. (c) 142. (b)

143. Inter Library Resource Centre (ILRC) is set up in the year:
   (a) 1972 (b) 1975
   (c) 1979 (d) 1982

144. National Medical Library of India is located at:
   (a) New Delhi (b) Kolkata
   (c) Bengaluru (d) Jhansi

145. What is ATIRA:
   (a) A name of CSIR laboratory
   (b) A name of DRDO laboratory
   (c) A name of SIET laboratory
   (d) UNESCO Pilot Project

146. CSIO is located at:
   (a) Gao (b) Chandigarh
   (c) Lucknow (d) New Delhi

147. What does ECOSOC stand for:
   (a) Economic and Social Council of the United Nations
   (b) Economic and Social Council of India
   (c) Economic and Social Council of India
   (d) Economic and Social Council of Japan

148. What is the periodicity of AGRINDEX:
   (a) Weekly (b) Monthly
   (c) Quarterly (d) Annual

149. VINITI is situated at Masco:
   (a) True (b) False

150. National Physical Laboratory is situated at:
   (a) Hyderabad (b) Ludhiana
   (c) New Delhi (d) Pune

Ans. : 143. (b) 144. (a) 145. (a) 146. (b)
147. (a) 148. (b) 149. (a) 150. (c)

151. What is DARE:
   (a) Referral Centre (b) Data Centre
   (c) IAC (d) Database
152. Match the following:

(1) ISI	(a) New Delhi
(2) ENVIS	(b) London
(3) DDC	(c) USA
(4) INSPEC	(d) Philadelphia
	(e) Pakistan

   Answers:
   (a) 1 (e), 2 (b), 3 (c), 4 (d)
   (b) 1 (a), 2 (c), 3 (b), 4 (d)
   (c) 1 (d), 2 (a), 3 (c), 4 (b)
   (d) 1 (d), 2 (a), 3 (b), 4 (c)
153. NISTADS stands for:
   (a) National Institute of Science & Technology Studies
   (b) National Institute of Science & Technology and Development Studies
   (c) NISST Database Services
   (d) NISSAT On-line Database Services
154. ISORID project is started by FID in:
   (a) 1972 (b) 1973
   (c) 1974 (d) 1975
155. Abbreviation UNISIST stands for:
   (a) United Nations Information System for Information Science
   (b) UNESCO Information Services for Science & Technology
   (c) United Nations Information System in Science & Technology
   (d) None of the above

Ans. : 151. (d) 152. (c) 153. (b) 154. (a)
155. (c)

156. The name of joint programme of UNESCO and ICSU is:
   (a) DELNET (b) NACID
   (c) ISORID (d) UNISIST

157. Copyright Bulletin is published from:
   (a) UK (b) USA
   (c) Moscow (d) Philadelphia

158. Central acquisition of foreign periodical project is being:
   (a) INSDOC (b) DST
   (c) CSIR (d) DESIDOC

159. Who is the publisher of 'Copyright Bulletin':
   (a) UNESCO (b) VINITI
   (c) ISI (d) ISO

160. ISORID stands for:
   (a) Institute for Research in Documentation
   (b) Institute System for Research in Documentation
   (c) International Information System on Research in Documentation
   (d) None of the above

161. NATIS programme is launched by:
   (a) ISCU (b) NISCAIR
   (c) NISSAT (d) UNESCO

162. General Information Programme (PGI) is started by:
   (a) UNISIST (b) UNESCO
   (c) SENDOC (d) NASSDOC

163. IAEA is:
   (a) An agency of UNO (b) An agency of FAO
   (c) An agency of WHO (d) None of these

Ans. : 156. (d) 157. (b) 158. (a) 159. (a) 160. (c) 161. (d) 162. (b) 163. (a)

164. What is the periodicity of INIS Atomindex?
    (a) Weekly (b) Monthly
    (c) Quarterly (d) Half yearly

165. INIS Atomindex is a publication of:
    (a) INIS (b) INIC
    (c) IAEA (d) All of the above

166. Who is the publisher of 'Informatics':
    (a) ILA (b) ALA
    (c) IFLA (d) UNESCO

167. Directory of Educational, documentation and information services is published by:
    (a) UNESCO (b) NISSAT
    (c) ICAR (d) NASSDOC

168. What does UNO stand for:
    (a) UNESCO Output
    (b) United Nations Organization
    (c) UNISIST Output
    (d) User Note

169. 'INIS Atomindex' was first published in:
    (a) May, 1970 (b) May, 1977
    (c) June, 1977 (d) June, 1979

170. Variable Energy Cylontron Centre is located at:
    (a) New Delhi (b) Mumbai
    (c) Kolkata (d) Bangalore

171. The VINITI was set up at Russia in the year:
    (a) 1952 (b) 1962
    (c) 1972 (d) 1982

Ans. : 164. (b) 165. (a) 166. (d) 167. (a) 168. (b) 169. (a) 170. (c) 171. (a)

172. 'Referativnyi Zhunal' is a publication of:
   (a) UNISIST (b) UNESCO
   (c) VINITI (d) INIS

173. Referativnyi Zhunal is a/an:
   (a) Indexing Periodical
   (b) Abstracting Periodical
   (c) Directory
   (d) Year Book

174. What is the periodicity of 'Hogi Nouki':
   (a) Weekly (b) Monthly
   (c) Half yearly (d) Annual

175. Match the following:

(1)	Atomindex	(a)	UNESCO
(2)	Informatics	(b)	AGRIS
(3)	Hogi Nauki	(c)	INIS
(4)	Copyright Bulletin	(d)	VINITI

   Answers:
   (a) 1 (c), 2 (a), 3 (c), 4 (d)
   (b) 1 (c), 2 (d), 3 (a), 4 (b)
   (c) 1 (c), 2 (a), 3 (d), 4 (b)
   (d) 1 (c), 2 (a), 3 (d), 4 (a)

176. 'Referativnyi Zhunal' was first published in:
   (a) 1953 (b) 1962
   (c) 1963 (d) 1973

177. NATIS programme is launched by UNESCO in the year:
   (a) 1962 (b) 1965
   (c) 1975 (d) 1977

Ans. : 172. (c) 173. (b) 174. (b) 175. (d)
176. (a) 177. (c)

178. Under which organization international Information Centre for Terminology functions:

(a) UNESCO (b) UNISIST

(c) ICSU (d) ISI

179. ISDS project is launched/ sponsored by:

(a) INSDOC (b) NISSAT

(c) UGC (d) UNISIST

180. What does ISDS stand for:

(a) International Serial Data System

(b) Indian Science Serial Data System

(c) International Scientific Serial Data System

(d) None of the above

181. UNISIST newsletter was first published in the year:

(a) 1962 (b) 1969

(c) 1972 (d) 1975

182. The abbreviation FAO stands for:

(a) Food Association

(b) Association for Food Organization

(c) Food and Agriculture Association

(d) Food and Agriculture Organization

183. AGRINDEX is a/an:

(a) Indexing periodical

(b) Abstracting periodical

(c) Indexing technique

(d) On-line technique

184. Who is the publisher of AGRINDEX:

(a) INIS (b) IISC

(c) CARIS (d) AGRIS

Ans. : 178. (b) 179. (d) 180. (a) 181. (c) 182. (d) 183. (a) 184. (d)

185. What is AGROVAC:
   (a) Database (b) Directory
   (c) Thesaurus (d) IAC

186. The name of a thesaurus, published by AGRIS is:
   (a) AGREX (b) AGROVOC
   (c) AGRINDEX (d) All of the above

187. Tropical Grain Legumes Information Centre is located at:
   (a) Nigeria (b) Paris
   (c) Delft (d) Colombo

188. Coconut Information Centre is located at:
   (a) Paris (b) Chicago
   (c) Germany (d) Shri Lanka

189. Match the following:

(1) ISRO	(a) Canada
(2) SARC	(b) Ahmedabad
(3) NIO	(c) Shri Lanka
(4) CISTI	(d) Goa

   Answers:
   (a) 1 (b), 2 (d), 3 (c), 4 (a)
   (b) 1 (b), 2 (c), 3 (d), 4 (a)
   (c) 1 (b), 2 (d), 3 (a), 4 (c)
   (d) 1 (c), 2 (b), 3 (a), 4 (d)

190. What is the name of FID earlier?
   (a) International Institute of Bibliography
   (b) Indian Association of Bibliography
   (c) International Association of Bibliography
   (d) Institute of Documentation

Ans. : 185. (c) 186. (b) 187. (a) 188. (d) 189. (b) 190. (a)

191. Semi-Arid Tropical Crops Documentation Centre is located at:

(a) India (b) USA

(c) Canada (d) Russia

192. 'World list of Library and Documentation Journals' is a publication of:

(a) NISCAIR (b) ALA

(c) FID (d) IFLA

193. Mark odd one: (clue: FID):

(a) Hennary La Fountain and Paul Otlet

(b) Allen Kant

(c) Derek De Solla Price

(d) All of the above

194. DIMDI is located at:

(a) Brussels (b) The Hague

(c) Canada (d) Germany

195. Who is the publisher of 'Directory of Indian Research in Indian Universities':

(a) UGC

(b) INSDOC

(c) Planning Commission

(d) Association of Indian Universities

196. Solid West Management is first published by INSDOC in the year:

(a) 1962 (b) 1972

(c) 1982 (d) 1992

Ans. : 191. (a) 192. (c) 193. (a) 194. (d) 195. (b) 196. (c)

197. 'Russian Scientific and Technical Publications: an accession list' is published by:
    (a) VINITI (b) RLIN
    (c) FID (d) INSDOC

198. Who is the publisher of 'A list of 2000 abstracting services in Science, Technology and Medicine':
    (a) INSDOC (b) FID
    (c) NLM (d) ICMR

199. Abbreviation DESIS stands for:
    (a) DESIDOC Information System
    (b) DRDO Scientific Information System
    (c) Defence Scientific Information System
    (d) Development Scientific Information System

200. The periodicity of APINESS newsletter is:
    (a) Weekly (b) Monthly
    (c) Quarterly (d) Annual

201. SIB stands for:
    (a) Bureau of Scientific Information
    (b) Scientific Information Bureau
    (c) State Bank of India
    (d) None of the above

202. SIET is located at:
    (a) Gujarat (b) Ahmedabad
    (c) Faridabad (d) Hyderabad

203. Under which organization DESIS functions:
    (a) DESIDOC (b) NASA
    (c) DRDO (d) BARC

Ans. : 197. (a) 198. (a) 199. (c) 200. (c)
201. (b) 202. (d) 203. (a)

204. What does TIC's stand for:
    (a) Tata Institute of CD-ROM
    (b) Tata Information Centre
    (c) Technical Information Service
    (d) Technical Information Centre's

205. Match the following:

(1) C-DAC	(a) Dept. of S & T
(2) NISSAT	(b) CMC, India
(3) INDONET	(c) Dept. of Electronic, India
(4) SENDOC	(d) SIET, Hyderabad

Answers:
    (a) 1 (a), 2 (b), 3 (c), 4 (d)
    (b) 1 (b), 2 (a), 3 (c), 4 (d)
    (c) 1 (c), 2 (a), 3 (b), 4 (d)
    (d) 1 (a), 2 (b), 3 (d), 4 (c)

206. The publisher of 'Guide to Book and journal Added' is:
    (a) NASSDOC (b) NISSAT
    (c) INSDOC (d) SENDOC

207. IACS is located at:
    (a) New Delhi (b) Kolkata
    (c) Mumbai (d) Madras

208. The periodicity of ILA Newsletter is:
    (a) Weekly (b) Fortnightly
    (c) Monthly (d) Quarterly

209. Who is the publisher of 'Annals of Library Science and Documentation'?
    (a) DRTC
    (b) Indian Library Association
    (c) IASLIC
    (d) INSDOC

Ans. : 204. (d) 205. (c) 206. (a) 207. (b) 208. (c) 209. (d)

210. The abbreviation of INPADOC is:
   (a) Indian Patent Documentation Centre
   (b) International Patent Documentation Centre
   (c) Indian National Patent Documentation Centre
   (d) Patent Documentation centre

211. INPADOC is located at:
   (a) Vienna, Austria (b) Delft, Netherland
   (c) Moscow, Russia (d) Philadelphia

212. The centers handling large volumes of data sometimes called as:
   (a) Information Center
   (b) Documentation Centre
   (c) Data Centre
   (d) Information Analysis Centre

213. Telephone conversation is an example of informal communication.
   (a) True (b) False

214. International Standardization Association was established in the year:
   (a) 1928 (b) 1929
   (c) 1938 (d) 1939

215. Committee on National Policy on Library and Information System was appointed in:
   (a) 1975 (b) 1985
   (c) 1988 (d) 1995

216. The book entitled 'Post war reconstruction of libraries' was written by:
   (a) W. Hulme (b) Melvil Dewey
   (c) W. C. B. Sayers (d) S. R. Ranganathan

Ans. : 210. (b) 211. (a) 212. (c) 213. (a)
214. (a) 215. (b) 216. (d)

217. MEDLINE is a/an:
   (a) Chemical Abstract
   (b) Indexing Tool
   (c) World Wide System
   (d) On-line retrieval system

218. National Translation Centre (NTC), UK is formerly known as:
   (a) L A Translation Centre
   (b) S L A Translation Centre
   (c) T L A Translation Centre
   (d) B L A Translation Centre

219. NICTAS is situated at:
   (a) Ahmedabad (b) Ludhiana
   (c) Kolkata (d) Keonjhar

220. ISO-2709 is the international standard format for bibliographic information interchange.
   (a) True (b) False

221. The year of establishment of NICTAS is:
   (a) 1942 (b) 1945
   (c) 1967 (d) 1986

222. UNIMARC is initiated by:
   (a) UNISIST (b) FID
   (c) IFLA (d) UNESCO

223. What does ICSU-AB stand for:
   (a) Indian Council of Scientific Union Abstracting Board
   (b) International Council of Scientific Union Abstracting Board
   (c) Indian Council of Scientific Union - A Board
   (d) None of the above

Ans. : 217. (d) 218. (b) 219. (a) 220. (a)
221. (d) 222. (c) 223. (b)

224. MARC-2 was set up in the year:
   (a) 1963 (b) 1965
   (c) 1966 (d) 1967

225. INSPEC is:
   (a) Indexing Technique
   (b) Abstracting Technique
   (c) Offline/Online retrieval service
   (d) Information Centre

226. 'Wealth of India' multi volume publication was brought by CSIR.
   (a) True (b) False

227. INRES is an example of:
   (a) Referral service
   (b) Reference service
   (c) Document Delivery service
   (d) Translation service

228. Match the following:
   (1) INPADOC (a) Ethopia
   (2) ISTI (b) Vienna
   (3) PADIS (c) China
   (4) NASA (d) USA

   Answers:
   (a) 1 (b), 2 (c), 3 (a), 4 (d)
   (b) 1 (d), 2 (a), 3 (c), 4 (b)
   (c) 1 (c), 2 (d), 3 (a), 4 (d)
   (d) 1 (b), 2 (a), 3 (c), 4 (b)

229. PASTIC is an information centre, situated at:
   (a) China (b) Russia
   (c) Pakistan (d) India

Ans. : 224. (d) 225. (c) 226. (a) 227. (a) 228. (a) 229. (c)

230. The year of establishment of National Standard Data System is:

(a) 1951 (b) 1958

(c) 1960 (d) 1963

231. 'Documentation, Bibliographic References Essential and Supplementary Elements' (1975) was published by:

(a) BSI (b) BIS

(c) ISO (d) NTIS

232. PADIS is located at:

(a) Pakistan (b) China

(c) Ethiopia (d) Vienna

233. PADIS stands for :

(a) Pan African Documentation and Information System

(b) Patent Documentation and Information System

(c) Pakistan Documentation and Information System

(d) None of the above

234. Match the following:

(1) NIC	(a) Thermo-physical Property
(2) IISC	(b) Medical Science
(3) NLM	(c) Information
(4) PIS	(d) Patent Information

Answers:

(a) 1 (a), 2 (b), 3 (b), 4 (d)

(b) 1 (d), 2 (a), 3 (b), 4 (b)

(c) 1 (c), 2 (d), 3 (b), 4 (a)

(d) 1 (c), 2 (a), 3 (b), 4 (d)

Ans. : **230. (d)** **231. (c)** **232. (c)** **233. (a)** **234. (d)**

235. Abbreviation ISTI stands for:

(a) Indian Institute of Science

(b) Indian Institute of Science & Technology

(c) Institute of Scientific & Technical Information

(d) Indian Institute of Scientific and Technical Information

236. ISTI is an example of:

(a) IAC (b) Information Centre

(c) Referral Centre (d) Clearing House

237. Institute of Scientific and Technical Information is located at:

(a) Chicago (b) Canada

(c) Colombo (d) China

238. What does INRES stands for:

(a) International Referral Service

(b) International Reference Service

(c) INSDOC Referral Service

(d) Indian Referral Service Centre

239. The year of establishment of Geographical Survey of India is:

(a) 1850 (b) 1851

(c) 1857 (d) 1859

240. IREDA stands for:

(a) Indian Referral Data Centre

(b) Information Retrieval Agency

(c) Indian Renewable Energy Development Agency

(d) None of these

Ans. : 235. (c) 236. (b) 237. (d) 238. (a)
239. (b) 240. (c)

241. Abbreviation DEVSIS stands for:
   (a) Scientific Development Information System
   (b) Development Scientific Information System
   (c) Development System for Scientific Information
   (d) Development Science Information System

242. Geographical Survey of India is situated at:
   (a) Kolkata (b) Mumbai
   (c) Lucknow (d) New Delhi

243. Defence Documentation Centre is an example of:
   (a) Information Centre (b) Data Centre
   (c) Lucknow (d) New Delhi

244. National Standard Reference Data System is set up by:
   (a) ANSI (b) ISI
   (c) ICSU (d) BIS

245. The year of establishment of NSRDS is:
   (a) 1956 (b) 1963
   (c) 1969 (d) 1974

246. NSRDS stands for:
   (a) National Standard Reference Data System
   (b) National Standard Referral Data System
   (c) NISSAT Reference Data System
   (d) National Standard Reference Data System

247. Match the following:

(1) UGC	(a) 1913
(2) CSIR	(b) 1942
(3) ICMR	(c) 1953
(4) ICAR	(d) 1911

Answers:
   (a) 1 (c), 2 (b), 3 (d), 4 (a)
   (b) 1 (c), 2 (b), 3 (a), 4 (d)
   (c) 1 (b), 2 (d), 3 (a), 4 (c)
   (d) 1 (b), 2 (c), 3 (d), 4 (a)

Ans. : 241. (d) 242. (a) 243. (c) 244. (c) 245. (b) 246. (a) 247. (a)

248. ERIC is a/an:
    (a) Referral Centre (b) Information Centre
    (c) Information Institution (d) IAC

249. What does ERIC stand for:
    (a) Education and Research in Canada
    (b) Education and Research Information Centre
    (c) Education and Research centre
    (d) Education Research Information Centre

250. 'De-silva's World Register of Trade' is an example of:
    (a) Trade Directory (b) Directory
    (c) National Directory (d) Bibliography

251. The abbreviation CODATA stands for:
    (a) Committee on Data for Applied Science
    (b) Committee on Data for Technical agency
    (c) Committee on Data for Technical Agency
    (d) Computerized Data

252. CRD stands for:
    (a) CODATA Referral Database
    (b) Computer Reference Database
    (c) Common Referral Database
    (d) Data for Critical Research

253. International Nuclear Information System is initiated by:
    (a) INIS (b) IAEA
    (c) DRDO (d) ARIC

254. The year of establishment of INIS is:
    (a) 1970 (b) 1972
    (c) 1975 (d) 1976

Ans. : 248. (a) 249. (d) 250. (a) 251. (c) 252. (a) 253. (b) 254. (a)

255. CAPS is an innovative Customized Information Service provided by:
   (a) SENDOC (b) NASSDOC
   (c) INSDOC (d) DESIDOC

256. Which one is the full form of ARIC:
   (a) Atomic Research and Information centre
   (b) Applied Research and Information Centre
   (c) Auto Research and Information Centre
   (d) Agriculture Research and Information Centre

257. Agriculture Research Institute, New Delhi is established in the year:
   (a) 1913 (b) 1943
   (c) 1967 (d) 1969

258. INIC stands for:
   (a) Indian Nuclear Information Centre
   (b) International Nuclear Information Centre
   (c) International Information Centre
   (d) National Information Centre

259. International Nuclear Information Centre is at:
   (a) The Hague (b) Peeking
   (c) Paris (d) Vienna

260. Abbreviation CISTI stands for:
   (a) Chain Indexing and Technical Information
   (b) Canada Institute for Scientific and Technical Information
   (c) China Institute for Scientific and Technical Information
   (d) None of the above

Ans. : 255. (c) 256. (d) 257. (c) 258. (b) 259. (d) 260. (b)

261. Scientific and Electronic Research Centre is at:
   (a) Lucknow (b) Bhopal
   (c) Madras (d) Rajasthan (Jaipur)

262. Match the following:

(1) ISDS	(a) Paris
(2) BANSD	(b) France
(3) IREDA	(c) New Delhi
(4) CNRS	(d) Bangladesh

   Answers:
   (a) 1 (a), 2 (d), 3 (d), 4 (c)
   (b) 1 (a), 2 (d), 3 (c), 4 (b)
   (c) 1 (b), 2 (c), 3 (d), 4 (a)
   (d) 1 (c), 2 (d), 3 (a), 4 (b)

263. Central Building Research Institute is situated at:
   (a) Roorkee (b) Ranchi
   (c) Kanpur (d) Indore

264. Industrial Toxicology Research Centre (ITRC) is at:
   (a) Lucknow (b) Varanasi
   (c) Jaipur (d) Jabalpur

265. Under which organization NEERI functions:
   (a) CSIR (b) ICSSR
   (c) NIC (d) NISSAT

266. National Botanical Research Institute(NBRI) is located at:
   (a) NOIDA (b) Lucknow
   (c) Pune (d) Patna

Ans. : 261. (c) 262. (b) 263. (a) 264. (a)
265. (a) 266. (b)

267. Indian Council of Agricultural Research at Pusa was shifted to New Delhi in the year:

(a) 1914 (b) 1919

(c) 1925 (d) 1929

268. Tata Fundamental and Industrial Research(TFIR) is at:

(a) Bangalore (Bengaluru) (b) Benares (Varanasi)

(c) Bombay (Mumbai) (d) Bhartpur

269. Which of the following organization provided document delivery service in UK:

(a) BTI (b) BLAISE

(c) BLDSC (d) JANET

270. Which of the following organization provided document delivery service in India:

(a) NIC (b) NISSAT

(c) NASSDOC (d) INSDOC

271. 'Index Translationum' is a publication of:

(a) UNISIST

(b) UNESCO

(c) INSDOC

(d) Library Association (UK)

272. The year of establishment of UNESCO is:

(a) 1945 (b) 1946

(c) 1947 (d) 1948

273. The Headquarter of UNESCO is at:

(a) Paris (b) Chicago

(c) New York (d) Delft

Ans. : 267. (d) 268. (c) 269. (c) 270. (d)
271. (b) 272. (b) 273. (a)

274. Match the following:

(1) NICLAI	(a) Lucknow
(2) NICFOS	(b) Mysore
(3) NICMAP	(c) Chennai
(4) NICDAP	(d) Bangalore

Answers:

(a) 1 (c), 2 (a), 3 (b), 4 (d)

(b) 1 (b), 2 (b), 3 (a), 4 (c)

(c) 1 (c), 2 (b), 3 (a), 4 (a)

(d) 1 (a), 2 (b), 3 (d), 4 (c)

275. Which one is the full form of NCSI:

(a) National Centre for Science Information

(b) National Institute of Scientific Information

(c) Nuclear Science Information Service

(d) International Nuclear Information Service

276. The abbreviation ICDE stands for:

(a) Indian Council for Education Development

(b) Indian Council for Distance Education

(c) Indian Council for Development

(d) International Council of Distance Education

277. CAS and SDI and examples of Alerting Service:

(a) True (b) False

278. Tata Energy Research Institute (TERI) is at:

(a) New Delhi (b) Hyderabad

(c) Ghaziabad (d) Trivandrum

Ans. : 274. (c) 275. (a) 276. (d) 277. (a) 278. (a)

279. Abbreviation TIFAC stands for:
    (a) Tata Institute of Food and Agriculture
    (b) Technical Information and Assessment Council
    (c) Technology, Information, Forecasting and Assessment Council
    (d) None of the above
280. NISSAT is the focal point in India for UNESCO/UNISIST programmes.
    (a) True (b) False
281. INFLIBNET is primarily cooperation networks of:
    (a) Public Libraries (b) Technical Libraires
    (c) University Libraries (d) Information Centers
282. The central agency for collection, classification and distribution of information in India is:
    (a) NISCAIR (b) NISSAT
    (c) NIC (d) DRTC
283. Medium Term Programme (MTP) is stared by:
    (a) IFLA (b) ALA
    (c) FID (d) LA (UK)
284. The first director of NASSDOC was:
    (a) V. K. R. V. Rao (b) B. S. Keshvan
    (c) N. M. Ketkar (d) S. R. Rangathan
285. Under which organization NASSDOC functions:
    (a) CSIR (b) ICSU
    (c) ICSSR (d) ICSR
286. Which among the following is not a NISSAT Sectorial Centre:
    (a) NICTAS (b) NICNET
    (c) NICHEM (d) NICMAP

Ans. : 279. (c) 280. (a) 281. (c) 282. (b) 283. (a) 284. (c) 285. (c) 286. (b)

287. Which of the following services is not offered by INSDOC:
   (a) Translation service
   (b) Abstracting and indexing services
   (c) Document delivery service
   (d) On-line information retrieval service

288. World Data Referral Centre is set up at Paris in the year:
   (a) 1973 (b) 1974
   (c) 1975 (d) 1976

289. International Buffalo Information Centre is located at:
   (a) Shri Lanka (b) Thailand
   (c) Germany (d) Italy

290. National Information Centre on Bibliographies is at:
   (a) New Delhi (b) Kolkata
   (c) Pune (d) Lucknow

291. NICOCD is located at:
   (a) New Delhi (b) Ahmedabad
   (c) Bangalore (d) Jaduguda Mines

292. National Information Centre on Crystallography (NICRYS) is:
   (a) New Delhi (b) Kolkata
   (c) Pune (d) Chennai

293. What does SIDO stand for:
   (a) Small Scale Industries Development Organization
   (b) Scientific Information Data Centre
   (c) Small Industries Centre
   (d) None of the above

Ans. : 287. (c) 288. (d) 289. (b) 290. (a)
291. (c) 292. (d) 293. (a)

294. National Information Centre on Advance Ceramics (NICAC) is situated at:

(a) Patna (b) Kolkata
(c) Kanpur (d) New Delhi

295. NDST stands for:

(a) National Data System
(b) National Data System for Science and Technology
(c) National Document Supply Centre
(d) National Document Supply & Service Centre

296. Which one is the full form of INFOTERM:

(a) Information Centre on Terminology
(b) UNISIST International Information Centre for Terminology
(c) International Information Centre for Terminology
(d) None of the above

297. National Information Centre for Compact Disc (NICOCD) is located at Bengaluru.

(a) True (b) False

298. Variable Energy Cyclotron Centre is situated at:

(a) Kolkata (b) NOIDA
(c) Meerut (d) Varanasi

299. Cassava Information Centre is at:

(a) Canada (b) Chicago
(c) Colombia (d) China

300. AGLIS is situated at:

(a) Vienna (b) Paris
(c) London (d) New Delhi

Ans. : 294. (b) 295. (c) 296. (b) 297. (a) 298. (a) 299. (c) 300. (d)

301. Match the following:

(1) NISCAIR	(a) Management
(2) SENDOC	(b) Industry
(3) NIC	(c) Bibliographic information

Answers:

(a) 1 (a), 2 (b), 3 (c) (b) 1 (c), 2 (b), 3 (b)
(c) 1 (c), 2 (b), 3 (a) (d) 1 (b), 2 (a), 3 (c)

302. The library and information service division of BARC is the National Centre for all INIS activities in India.
(a) True (b) False

303. The centenary of the FID was celebrated in the year:
(a) 1975 (b) 1985
(c) 1993 (d) 1995

304. The present Director General of ICAR is:
(a) Dr. Mangala Rao (b) Dr. S. Ayyappan
(c) D. B. Barua (d) Dr. Panjab Singh

305. The present Director General of CSIR is:
(a) Dr. R. A. Mashelkar
(b) Dr. Mangala Rao
(c) Dr. Panjab Singh
(d) Prof. Samir K. Brahmachari

306. Who is the present Director General of ICMR?
(a) D. B. Barua
(b) Dr. Vishwa Mohan Katoch
(c) Prof Nirmal K. Gangulee
(d) Dr. Mangala Roa

307. The present Chairman of ICSSR is:
(a) Dr. Punjab Singh (b) Dr. P. R. Goswami
(c) Prof. Javed Alam (d) None of the above

Ans. : 301. (c) 302. (a) 303. (d) 304. (b)
305. (d) 306. (b) 307. (c)

308. CSIR is an apex body for the promotion of research in Science & Technology in India.
   (a) True (b) False
309. The head of NASSDOC is designated as:
   (a) Librarian (b) Chairman
   (c) Director (d) Chief Librarian
310. The premier institution for prescribing stands in India is:
   (a) Bureau of Indian Standards
   (b) University Grants Commission
   (c) Indian Standard Institute
   (d) Indian Standard Council
311. IFIS stands for:
   (a) Indian Food Information System
   (b) International Food Information System
   (c) Indian Foreign Information System
   (d) INFROSS Information Service
312. NICOROM is a sectrol information centre related to:
   (a) Bibliomatrics (b) Drug research
   (c) Management (d) CD-ROM
313. UNESCO's information programme is known as:
   (a) Universal Bibliographic control
   (b) National Information Service
   (c) General Information Programme
   (d) Universal Availability of Publication

Ans. : 308. (a) 309. (c) 310. (a) 311. (b) 312. (d) 313. (c)

314. Mass Communication Research Centre (MCRC) at Jamia Millia Islamia, New Delhi was established in 1982 with cooperation of Canadian International Development Agency and York University of Canada.

(a) True (b) False

315. Indian Institute of Mass Communication (IIMC) was established in:

(a) 1962 (b) 1965
(c) 1972 (d) 1985

316. CONSER stands for:

(a) Conservation of Books
(b) Conversation of Books
(c) Conversion of Serials
(d) Conservation of Periodicals

317. 'Patent Watch Service' was provided by:

(a) INSDOC (b) SENDOC
(c) PTI (d) BARC

318. INTEXT project was launched by:

(a) DST & NIC
(b) Documentation and IGNOU
(c) Doordarshan and NIC
(d) IGNOU

319. DESIDOC Transidex is an index of:

(a) Periodicals (b) Translation
(c) Newspapers (d) All of the above

320. The author of the book 'Little Science, Big Scinece' is:

(a) Eric De Solla Price (b) J. Thomson
(c) Alvin Toffler (d) Bill Gates

Ans. : 314. (a) 315. (b) 316. (c) 317. (a) 318. (c) 319. (b) 320. (a)

321. Match the following:

(1) Lexicon	(a) Greek
(2) Index	(b) Latin
(3) Vocabulary	(c) Latin
(4) Encyclopedia	(d) Greek

Answers:

(a) 1 (a), 2 (b), 3 (c), 4 (d)

(b) 1 (a), 2 (c), 3 (d), 4 (b)

(c) 1 (b), 2 (c), 3 (d), 4 (a)

(d) 1 (b), 2 (c), 3 (a), 4 (d)

322. 'Sociological Abstracts' is published how many times in a year:

(a) 2 (b) 4

(c) 5 (d) 7

323. Data India published by Press Institute of India, New Delhi is weekly publication.

(a) True (b) False

324. GRANTHAGAR (Bengal) 1937 published by:

(a) ILA (b) IASLIC

(c) Delhi Library Association

(d) Bengal Library Association

325. 'Bio Systematic Index' is found in:

(a) Biological Index (b) Biological Abstract

(c) Chemical Abstract (d) Genetic Index

326. A sheet of book paper folder once, making two leaves of 4 pages called:

(a) Micro Fiche (b) Standard Page

(c) Folio (d) None of the above

Ans. : 321. (a) 322. (c) 323. (a) 324. (d) 325. (b) 326. (c)

327. Which kind of bibliography is a systematic list of all the books published all over the world?

(a) Title (b) Author

(c) Trade (d) Universal

328. 'Directory of National Bibliography' edited by S. P. Sen is in 4 volumes, covering persons from all works of life.

(a) True (b) False

329. Index of the "Times of India" is published from:

(a) London, UK (b) Kolkata

(c) Mumbai (d) Chennai

330. In 1958, Indian Society for Plant Physiology was established at:

(a) Delhi (b) Kolkata

(c) Varanasi (d) Agra

331. Indian Council of Social Science Research(ICSSR) was established in 1969.

(a) True (b) False

332. National Council of Applied Economic Research was established in................in 1956.

(a) NOIDA (b) Chennai

(c) New Delhi (d) Kharagpur

333. International Information Centre for Terminology (INFOTERM), established in year:

(a) 1972 (b) 1975

(c) 1977 (d) 1979

334. The first notable index is:

(a) Index Medicus (b) Biological Index

(c) Index India (d) Poole's Index

Ans. :	327. (d)	328. (c)	329. (a)	330. (a)
	331. (a)	332. (c)	333. (a)	334. (d)

335. 'Current Library & Information Science' is a publication of:
   (a) AGRIS (b) AGLIS
   (c) ICAR (d) CSIR
336. Who is the present Director of NASSDOC:
   (a) Dr. Jadish Arora (b) R. A. Mashelkar
   (c) P. R. Goswami (d) Dr. H. K. Kaul
337. 'Directory of Special and Research libraries in India 1985' was published by:
   (a) IASLIC (b) DESIDOC
   (c) SENDOC (d) SLA
338. 'India: A Reference Annual' is a:
   (a) A Statistical Digest (b) Directory
   (c) An Encyclopaedia (d) Year Book
339. To find out the name of present Railway Minister of India, appropriate source of information is:
   (a) Who was who of India
   (b) India Who's who
   (c) Dictionary of National Biography
   (d) None of the above

Ans. : 335. (b) 336. (c) 337. (a) 338. (d) 339. (b)

4

Research and Statistical Methods

1. 'Method means the logical process used in discovering or in demonstrating the truth' said by:
   (a) Aristotle (b) G. K. Zipf
   (c) C. Shannon (d) Cossa
2. 'Science goes with the method, not with the subject matter' said by:
   (a) Newton (b) Stuart Chase
   (c) H. E. Bliss (d) Bradford
3. What does KM stand for:
   (a) Keyboard (b) Kilo Miter
   (c) Knowledge Management (d) Karl Marks
4. Panel Survey method is a direct extension of:
   (a) Interview sampling (b) Case study
   (c) Sampling technique (d) Data collection

Ans. : 1. (d) 2. (b) 3. (c) 4. (a)

5. In Research Design which is considered as the most important component:
   (a) Case study
   (b) Review of literature
   (c) Observation
   (d) Formation of hypothesis
6. In Historical Method of research, data collection is done through using questionnaire technique.
   (a) True (b) False
7. The third step of Research Methodology is:
   (a) Selection and analysis of problem
   (b) Data Collection
   (c) Analysis of Data
   (d) Report Writing
8. Which of the following is the research tool:
   (a) Interview (b) Questionnaire
   (c) Both (a) and (b) (d) None of the above
9. The characteristic of research is:
   (a) Continuous process
   (b) Systematic
   (c) Follow Rigorous standards
   (d) All the above
10. Mark the odd one:
   (a) Experimental research design
   (b) Diagnostic research design
   (c) Exploratory research design
   (d) Applied research design

Ans. : 5. (d) 6. (b) 7. (c) 8. (c) 9. (d) 10. (d)

11. 'Einstein's theory of relativity' is an example of:
    (a) Historical research
    (b) Seminal research
    (c) Fundamental research
    (d) Experimental research
12. 'Spiral of Scientific Method' is an example of:
    (a) Pure research (b) Historical research
    (c) Inductive research (d) Deductive research
13. Who defines that 'knowledge is the consequence of a filterized process through intellectual system':
    (a) J. H. Shera (b) Ackaff
    (c) B. Lamare (d) S. R. Ranganathan
14. 'Knowledge is a sum total of information conserved by civilization' said by:
    (a) Ackaff (b) A. J. Lotka
    (c) Karl Marx (d) S. R. Ranganathan
15. Match the following:
    (1) Data (a) Cotton
    (2) Information (b) Yarn
    (3) Knowledge (c) Cloth
    Answers:
    (a) 1 (a), 2 (b), 3 (c) (b) 1 (b), 2 (a), 3 (c)
    (c) 1 (a), 2 (c), 3 (b) (d) 1 (c), 2 (b), 3 (a)
16. Scientific method of research can be used:
    (a) Only in humanities (b) Only in science
    (c) Only in social science (d) In all the disciplines

Ans. : 11. (b) 12. (c) 13. (a) 14. (d)
15. (a) 16. (d)

17. Historical method of research can be applied:
    (a) Only in history (b) Only in humanities
    (c) Only in science (d) In all the disciplines
18. Experimental research is:
    (a) Present oriented research
    (b) Future oriented research
    (c) Free-fundamental research
    (d) Priori oriented research
19. Survey research is:
    (a) Present oriented research
    (b) Future oriented research
    (c) Priori oriented research
    (d) Free-fundamental research
20. Research starts from Nadir and ends at:
    (a) Nadir (b) Zenith
    (c) Ascendant (d) Descendant
21. The famous book 'Logic' was written by Hegel and published in the year:
    (a) 1800 (b) 1812
    (c) 1847 (d) 1849
22. The main step of Scientific Method is:
    1. Selection and analysis of problem
    2. Formulation of Hypothesis
    3. Data Collection
    4. Preparation of report

    Answer :

    (a) 1, 3, 4 (b) 2, 3, 4
    (c) 1, 2, 3 (d) All the above

Ans. : 17. (d) 18. (b) 19. (a) 20. (a) 21. (b) 22. (d)

23. Who define that 'Design is the process of making decision before the situation arises in which the decision is to be carried out:
    (a) Hegal (b) A. L. Edward
    (c) Ackaff (d) S. R. Ranganathan
24. Formal and Informal Text are carried out in:
    (a) Diagnostic research design
    (b) Experimental research design
    (c) Exploratory research design
    (d) Applied research design
25. Academic object and Utilitarian object are two folds of:
    (a) Social science research
    (b) Applied research
    (c) Seminal research
    (d) Content analysis research
26. Normative principles is given by Ranganathan, it is based on:
    (a) Historical research (b) Scientific research
    (c) Survey research (d) Statistical research
27. What is hypothesis?
    (a) A tentative
    (b) Plan of study
    (c) An important instrument of research
    (d) All the above
28. Null Hypothesis is started:
    (a) Negatively (b) Positively
    (c) Both 'a' and 'b' (d) Neither 'a' and 'b'

Ans. : 23. (c) 24. (a) 25. (a) 26. (b) 27. (d) 28. (a)

29. Who define that 'Hypothesis is suggested answer to a problem':
    (a) J. B. Best (b) C. W. Cleverdon
    (c) Town Sand (d) A. L. Edward
30. 'A hypothesis is a nature of the relationship between two or more variable, it is an alternative answer to the question' said by:
    (a) Town Sand (b) A. L. Edward
    (c) S. R. Ranganathan (d) J. B. Best
31. The famous book 'The Republic' was written by:
    (a) Ackaff (b) Aristotle
    (c) Plato (d) Karl Marx
32. Who discovered the concept of Zero?
    (a) Karl Marx (b) Plato
    (c) Aryabhatta (d) Vivekanand
33. The concept of Fundamental Categories is enunciated by:
    (a) J. H. Shera (b) F. Rider
    (c) Melvil Dewey (d) S. R. Ranganathan
34. Science is a systematized positive knowledge or that branch of study which is concerned with a connected body of demonstrated truth.
    (a) Truth (b) False
35. Who defines that 'Science is partially unified knowledge':
    (a) Plato (b) Marx
    (c) Edward (d) Ranganathan

Ans. :	29. (c)	30. (b)	31. (c)	32. (c)
	33. (d)	34. (a)	35. (a)	

36. Match the following:

(1) Experimental Research	(a) Cranfield studies
(2) Applied Research	(b) Five laws of library science
(3) Inductive Research	(c) Chain procedure
(4) Fundamental Research	(d) Spiral of scientific method

Answers:

(a) 1 (a), 2 (c), 3 (d), 4 (b)

(b) 1 (a), 2 (b), 3 (c), 4 (d)

(c) 1 (a), 2 (b), 3 (d), 4 (c)

(d) 1 (a), 2 (c), 3 (b), 4 (d)

37. 'Controlled Group' is a term, which is used in:

(a) Interview method

(b) Scientific research

(c) Survey research

(d) Experimental research

38. Delphi Technique is related with:

(a) Data analysis (b) Data collection

(c) Data dissemination (d) Data processing

39. 'Ramanujum theory of Mathematics' is an example of:

(a) Bibliomatrics method (b) Historical method

(c) Seminal research (d) Scientific research

40. Who is the author of 'Leviathan'?

(a) Thomas Hobbes (b) H. Spencer

(c) P. Louis (d) R. F. Clark

41. Who is the father of Liberalism?

(a) Bradford (b) John Locke

(c) Thomas Hobbes (d) Ranganathan

Ans. : 36. (a) 37. (d) 38. (b) 39. (c) 40. (a) 41. (b)

42. Who is the father of Absolution?
   (a) Thomas Hobbes (b) A. L. Edward
   (c) B. Lemarc (d) S. R. Ranganathan
43. Which of the following technique is not employed in Bibliomatrics?
   (a) Ranking (b) Citing
   (c) Counting (d) Measuring
44. British Association for Advertisement of Science is located at:
   (a) Paris (b) Chicago
   (c) Cambridge (d) London
45. The book 'Classification of Sciences' was written by:
   (a) Charles Darwin (b) Bacon
   (c) Herbert Spencer (d) Ranganathan
46. Philosophy means:
   (a) Love of wisdom
   (b) Love without wisdom
   (c) Love of Society
   (d) None of the above
47. Philosophy is the apex of the pyramid of knowledge.
   (a) True (b) False
48. Who is the author of 'Advances of Learning':
   (a) Socrates (b) Plato
   (c) Peter Louis (d) Francis Bacon
49. 'Social Sciences are concerned with the laws that given society and social development of man' said by:
   (a) Aristotle (b) Socrates
   (c) Peter Louis (d) Charles Darwin

Ans. :	42. (a)	43. (d)	44. (c)	45. (c)
	46. (a)	47. (a)	48. (d)	49. (c)

50. The author of the book 'Social Contract' is:
    (a) Peter Louis (b) A. L. Edward
    (c) J. J. Roussean (d) Francis Bacon

51. The year of establishment of 'Asiatic Society of Calcutta' is:
    (a) 1684 (b) 1912
    (c) 1884 (d) 1784

52. Cluster was formerly known as Subject Bundle.
    (a) True (b) False

53. 'Historical research is the application of the scientific method of inquiry to historical problems' said by:
    (a) A. J. Wood (b) J. B. Best
    (c) Mouley (d) W. H. George

54. Who define that 'Historical method of research is a system or right procedure for attainment of historical truth':
    (a) Allen Kent (b) Alan Pritchard
    (c) Clavin Mooers (d) Richard F. Clark

55. 'Man is mortal, Shyam is a man, Shyam is mortal' this is an example of:
    (a) Deductive reasoning (b) Seminal research
    (c) Deduction (d) Historical research

56. Bradford's law and Zipf's law are used as:
    (a) Citation analysis
    (b) Rank frequency analysis of data
    (c) System analysis
    (d) None of these

Ans. : 50. (c) 51. (d) 52. (a) 53. (b) 54. (d) 55. (a) 56. (b)

57. Agglomeration was formerly known as:
    (a) Dissection
    (b) Cluster
    (c) Subject Bundle
    (d) Partial Comprehension

58. Who gives rise to formation of Compound Subject:
    (a) Laminatin (b) Fusion
    (c) Fission (d) Cluster

59. According to Dr. S. R. Ranganathan 'When the basic layer is a basic subject and the other layers are isolate idea, a .... subject is formed':
    (a) Basic (b) Compound
    (c) Complex (d) Pure

60. Statistics for lawyer refers to:
    (a) General relation (b) Influence relation
    (c) Bias relation (d) Tool relation

61. Match the following:

(1) Pure subject	(a) Fusion
(2) Basic subject	(b) Distillation
(3) Compound subject	(c) Loose Assemblage
(4) Complex subject	(d) Lamination

    Answers:
    (a) 1 (a), 2 (b), 3 (c), 4 (d)
    (b) 1 (b), 2 (a), 3 (d), 4 (c)
    (c) 1 (a), 2 (b), 3 (d), 4 (c)
    (d) 1 (b), 2 (a), 3 (c), 4 (d)

Ans. : 57. (d) 58. (a) 59. (b) 60. (c)
61. (b)

62. What is the process of division or breaking up into parts:
(a) Dissection (b) Denudation
(c) Fission (d) Fusion

63. 'Agriculture of wheat' is an example of:
(a) Compound subject
(b) Primary Basic subject
(c) Pure subject
(d) Complex subject

64. 'Cataloguing in libraries' is an example of:
(a) Basic subject
(b) Compound subject
(c) Complex subject
(d) Primary Basic subject

65. 'Urban Female' is an example of:
(a) Pure subject (b) Compound Subject
(c) Complex subject (d) Basic subject

66. What is the process of collecting to-gather of entities into larger masses without cohesion among the components?
(a) Lamination (b) Fusion
(c) Fission (d) Agglomeration

67. 'Political Science' is:
(a) Basic subject
(b) Primary Basic subject
(c) Compound subject
(d) Complex subject

Ans. : 62. (c) 63. (a) 64. (b) 65. (b) 66. (d) 67. (a)

68. Nipponology is an example of:
    (a) Lamination (b) Distillation
    (c) Agglomeration (d) Cluster
69. Statistical Analysis is an example of:
    (a) Dissection (b) Denudation
    (c) Distillation (d) Lamination
70. Subject is a systematic and organized body of ideas.
    (a) True (b) False
71. The famous book 'Das Capital' is written by:
    (a) Aristotle (b) Karl Marx
    (c) Max Weber (d) Francis Bacon
72. What is the author of 'City of God':
    (a) Margaret Mann (b) Socrates
    (c) Donkar Deyvis (d) Thomas Acquinas
73. Theory of Evolution was first propounded by:
    (a) B. Lemare (b) C. Shannan
    (c) Karl Marx (d) Max Weber
74. The word 'Bibliomatrics' was first used by Allan Pritchard in the year 1969.
    (a) True (b) False
75. 'Bibliomatrics' is a study of:
    (a) Bibliotherapy
    (b) Bio-technology
    (c) Mathematics for librarianship
    (d) Mathematics for Bio-physics

Ans. :	68. (d)	69. (c)	70. (a)	71. (b)
	72. (d)	73. (a)	74. (a)	75. (c)

76. Which of the following techniques, employed in Bibliomatrics:
    (a) Counting
    (b) Citation analysis
    (c) Rank and size frequency distribution
    (d) All the above

77. Match the following:

(1) History	(a) Fusion
(2) Indology	(b) Cluster
(3) Bio-physics	(c) Agglomeration
(4) Natural Sciences	(d) Distillation

Answers:
    (a) 1 (a), 2 (b), 3 (c), 4 (d)
    (b) 1 (d), 2 (b), 3 (a), 4 (c)
    (c) 1 (b), 2 (c), 3 (a), 4 (d)
    (d) 1 (c), 2 (b), 3 (a), 4 (d)

78. Law of sampling is related with:
    (a) Law of statistical regularity
    (b) Law of India
    (c) Both (a) and (b)
    (d) Neither 'a' and 'b'

79. Law of Scattering is described by:
    (a) Bradford (b) G. K. Zipf
    (c) A. J. Lotka (d) Claudes Sharman

80. INFORSS stands for:
    (a) Information Retrieval System
    (b) Information Requirement of Social Sciences
    (c) Information Retrieval System for Social Sciences
    (d) Information Requirement for Sciences

Ans. : 76. (d) 77. (b) 78 (c) 79. (a) 80. (b)

81. INFORSS is one of the major user's studies conducted in UK.
    (a) True (b) False

82. Cranfield Tests was described by:
    (a) C. W. Cleverdon (b) Fermont Rider
    (c) G. K. Zipf (d) A. J. Lotka

83. Bio-technology is an example of:
    (a) Lamination (b) Dissection
    (c) Fission (d) Fusion

84. Match the following:
    (1) Authority centered thinking (a) Max Weber
    (2) Positivistic thinking (b) Aristotle
    (3) Speculative thinking (c) August Compte

    Answers:
    (a) 1 (a), 2 (b), 3 (c) (b) 1 (a), 2 (c), 3 (b)
    (c) 1 (b), 2 (c), 3 (a) (d) 1 (b), 2 (a), 3 (c)

85. The bibliographical and type studies carried out in:
    (a) Cranfield test (b) Case study
    (c) Historical studies (d) Four cell studies

86. Match the following:
    (1) Management (a) Agglomeration
    (2) Humanities (b) Cluster
    (3) Oceanography (c) Distillation
    (4) Astrophysics (d) Fusion

    Answers:
    (a) 1 (a), 2 (c), 3 (b), 4 (d)
    (b) 1 (c), 2 (a), 3 (b), 4 (d)
    (c) 1 (c), 2 (d), 3 (b), 4 (a)
    (d) 1 (a), 2 (b), 3 (b), 4 (d)

Ans. : 81. (a) 82. (a) 83. (d) 84. (a)
85. (b) 86. (b)

87. 'Tree of porphyry' is formed as result of Dichotomy.
    (a) True (b) False

88. Which of the following is the characteristic of hypothesis:
    (a) Should be tested (b) Should be economic
    (c) Should be conceptual (d) All the above

89. Which of the following is the function of hypothesis:
    (a) Help in theory construction
    (b) As a source of methodology
    (c) As an organizing principle
    (d) All the above

90. 'Earth is round', it is an example of:
    (a) Conceptual hypothesis
    (b) Universal hypothesis
    (c) Experimental hypothesis
    (d) Non-experimental hypothesis

91. The study of past is related to:
    (a) Experimental method of research
    (b) Survey method of research
    (c) Historical method of research
    (d) Spiral of scientific research

92. 'Grey Literature' means:
    (a) Literature which is semi-published
    (b) Literature which is to be published in future
    (c) Documents which are bound in grey cloth
    (d) Literature which contains classified information

Ans. : 87. (a) 88. (d) 89. (b) 90. (c)
91. (c) 92. (a)

93. Flow of information goes from:
    (a) Bottom to top (b) Top to bottom
    (c) Middle to bottom (d) Middle to top
94. The term 'Truncation' is used in:
    (a) Coordination (b) Budgeting
    (c) Search formulation (d) Thesaurus
95. The basic communication model was developed by:
    (a) Socrates (b) Plato
    (c) Charles Darwin (d) Aristotle
96. Knowledge is the organized form of information:
    (a) True (b) False
97. Indicate the name of the philosopher, who was the exponent of Scientific Method:
    (a) S. R. Ranganthan (b) Aristotle
    (c) F. W. Taylor (d) Bacon
98. A research proceeds from general to specific is:
    (a) Inductive logic (b) Deductive logic
    (c) Both 'a' and 'b' (d) None of the above
99. A research proceeds from specific to general is:
    (a) Inductive logic (b) Deductive logic
    (c) Both 'a' and 'b' (d) None of the above
100. Observation method is not used in:
    (a) Case study
    (b) Quantitative research
    (c) Conceptual research
    (d) Historical research

Ans. :	93. (b)	94. (c)	95. (d)	96. (a)
	97. (d)	98. (b)	99. (a)	100. (d)

101. The questions, where answers are already quoted to be chosen, are called:
    (a) Open ended questions
    (b) Close ended questions
    (c) Procoded
    (d) None of these

102. DISISS stands for:
    (a) Information services in Social Sciences
    (b) Design of Information Service in the Social Sciences
    (c) Defence Information Service
    (d) None of these

103. Four important techniques used in explore the information need of users are:
    (a) Report, Questionnaire, Investigation, Observation
    (b) Dairy, Questionnaire, Investigation, Observation
    (c) Dairy, Questionnaire, Interview, Observation
    (d) None of the above

104. Which is the following research method is useful in a study on measuring the active life of periodicals:
    (a) Case Study
    (b) Interview
    (c) Survey
    (d) Citation analysis

105. 'Decachotomy' refers to a division into:
    (a) 2
    (b) 10
    (c) 100
    (d) None of the above

106. 'Dichotomy' refers to a division into:
    (a) 2
    (b) 10
    (c) 100
    (d) Many

Ans. : 101. (c) 102. (a) 103. (c) 104. (c) 105. (b) 106. (a)

107. 'Polychotomy' refers to a division into:
   (a) 2 (b) 10
   (c) 100 (d) Many

108. In a research report/ paper to refer to an immediate reference, the following term is used:
   (a) Ibid (b) Op. cit
   (c) Loc. cit (d) None of the above

109. In a research report/paper to refer to an earlier but not immediate preceding reference, the term used:
   (a) Ibid (b) Op. cit
   (c) Loc. cit (d) None of the above

110. 'Knowledge in the modern information age is the central capital, the cost centre and the crucial resources of the economy' said by:
   (a) J. H. Shera (b) S. R. Ranganathan
   (c) Peter Drucker (d) H. E. Bliss

111. Inkblot test is developed by:
   (a) L. Guttman (b) A. Pritchard
   (c) Allen Kent (d) H. Rorschach

112. Which of the following method of research and useful study on measuring the action life periodical:
   (a) Cluster sampling (b) Citation analysis
   (c) Experiment (d) Survey

113. Conversion of Response into a set of number is called:
   (a) Coding (b) Cataloguing
   (c) Classification (d) Number setting

Ans. : 107. (d) 108. (a) 109. (b) 110. (c)
111. (d) 112. (b) 113. (a)

114. A foot note is:
   (a) A supplementary information to text
   (b) A bibliographical reference
   (c) Both 'a' and 'd'
   (d) None of the above

115. Mean, Median and Modes are measures of central tendency.
   (a) True (b) False

116. Research report is an account of:
   (a) Only Conclusion
   (b) Only Suggestion
   (c) Data analysis
   (d) Research work with conclusion and suggestion

117. Result 30 items out of 60 is a .... statistics:
   (a) Sampling (b) Inferential
   (c) Descriptive (d) Time series

118. A systematic organization of data in column and rows is called:
   (a) Coding (b) Graphs
   (c) Data collection (d) Tabulation

119. Diagrams and graphs were used in statistic first by .... fair in 1762:
   (a) William Play (b) A. Pritchard
   (c) Kautilya (d) M. Weber

120. Spiral means:
   (a) Research process (b) A research tool
   (c) A process (d) An unending circle

Ans. : 114. (c) 115. (a) 116. (d) 117. (b) 118. (d) 119. (a) 120. (d)

121. The study aimed at finding out best method of charging of book is:
(a) Relay research (b) Applied research
(c) Experimental research (d) Basic research

122. A research design should not include:
(a) Hypothesis (b) Methodology
(c) Findings (d) Scope

123. Bibliographic coupling is a:
(a) Identification of document
(b) Technique for identify theme of document from its citation
(c) Identification of author of document
(d) None of the above

124. Scalogram Analysis was devised by:
(a) Bogardus (b) Eckhendt
(c) Plato (d) Louis Guttman

125. Systematic Sampling is also known as:
(a) Interval sampling (b) Cluster sampling
(c) Random sampling (d) Stratified sampling

126. The book 'Motivation factor a theory of personnel management' is authored by:
(a) Max Weber & A. Hezeberg
(b) Martin and Lorry A. Bruskemp
(c) Peter Drucker & M. Weber
(d) P. Drucker & Martin

Ans. : 121. (b) 122. (c) 123. (b) 124. (d)
125. (a) 126. (b)

127. During Vedic Period, Universe of knowledge is divided into:
    (a) Dharma, Darshan, Kama and Sahitya
    (b) Dharma, Kama, Darshan and Moksha
    (c) Dharma, Karma, Kama and Moksha
    (d) Dharma, Karma, Darshan and Moksha

128. A subject without any isolate idea:
    (a) Generic Subject (b) Complex Subject
    (c) Compound Subject (d) Basic Subject

Ans. : 127. (c) 128. (d)

5

Information Processing and Retrieval Techniques

1. What was the earlier name of National Library of India?
   (a) Asiatic Society Library
   (b) The Royal Library
   (c) Calcutta Public Library
   (d) Imperial Library of Calcutta
2. Classification language is a/an:
   (a) Artificial language (b) Natural language
   (c) Common language (d) Difficult language
3. APUPA method is related to:
   (a) Cataloguing (b) Classification
   (c) Documentation (d) Referral service
4. Seminal Mnemonics are found in:
   (a) LC (b) BC
   (c) CC (d) UDC

Ans. : 1. (d) 2. (a) 3. (b) 4. (c)

5. Classifier is one who is a/an:
   (a) Eminent scholar for classification
   (b) One who devises classification scheme
   (c) Both (a) and (b)
   (d) None of the above

6. Margaret Mann is known for contribution in:
   (a) Computerization (b) Cataloguing
   (c) Classification (d) Library Management

7. In the opinion of Ranganathan the basic subjects are formed by:
   (a) Fission (b) Fusion
   (c) Denudation (d) Division

8. Who was the chief architect of the dynamic theory of library classification?
   (a) H. E. Bliss (b) J. D. Brown
   (c) Dr. Ranganathan (d) Richardson

9. Law of local variation is one of the .... as formulated by Dr. S. R. Ranganathan:
   (a) Canons (b) Principles
   (c) Basic laws (d) Five laws

10. The country in which the library is located, dubbed as (in classification):
    (a) Library country (b) Mother country
    (c) Favored country (d) None of the above

11. Which of the following is an isolate:
    (a) History (b) Law
    (c) America (USA) (d) Psychology

Ans. : 5. (d) 6. (c) 7. (a) 8. (a) 9. (c) 10. (b) 11. (c)

12. Dr. S. R. Ranganathan enunciated 9 steps in classifying a document.
    (a) True (b) False
13. The classes belonging to the same are termed as:
    (a) Canonical classes (b) Co-ordinate classes
    (c) Subordinate classes (d) Basic classes
14. The device that makes use of initial alphabets in sharpening a class number:
    (a) Initial device (b) Sharpening device
    (c) Geographical device (d) Alphabetical device
15. BSO is:
    (a) Cataloguing code (b) Exchange format
    (c) Classification scheme (d) None of the above
16. The 'Book number' system devised by Dr. Ranganathan has been given in Colon Classification.
    (a) True (b) False
17. One who designs a scheme of classification is known as:
    (a) Classifier (b) Classificationist
    (c) Book Classifier (d) All of the above
18. The classification of the things according to size, colour etc. is called:
    (a) Library classification
    (b) Natural classification
    (c) Logical classification
    (d) Artificial classification
19. In logic classification the basis of division is:
    (a) Science (b) Logic
    (c) Philosophy (d) Logic and Philosophy

Ans. :	12. (a)	13. (b)	14. (d)	15. (c)
	16. (a)	17. (b)	18. (d)	19. (d)

20. Match the following:

(1) CC	(a) Ranganathan
(2) UDC	(b) Brown
(3) DDC	(c) FID
(4) SC	(d) Dewey

Answers:

(a) 1 (a), 2 (b), 3 (c), 4 (d)

(b) 1 (a), 2 (c), 3 (d), 4 (b)

(c) 1 (a), 2 (c), 3 (b), 4 (d)

(d) 1 (a), 2 (c), 3 (d), 4 (d)

21. Match the following:

(1) UDC	(a) 1904
(2) LC	(b) 1905
(3) Subject Classification	(c) 1906
(4) Colon Classification	(d) 1933

Answers:

(a) 1 (a), 2 (b), 3 (c), 4 (d)

(b) 1 (a), 2 (c), 3 (b), 4 (d)

(c) 1 (a), 2 (c), 3 (d), 4 (b)

(d) 1 (b), 2 (a), 3 (c), 4 (d)

22. Henry La Fontaine is related with:

(a) CC (b) EC

(c) BC (d) UDC

23. The recent general classification scheme published by FID in 1978 is:

(a) DDC (b) UDC

(c) BSO (d) EC

Ans. : 20. (b) 21. (d) 22. (d) 23. (c)

24. Classification Research Group (U.K.) was founded in:
    (a) 1952 (b) 1958
    (c) 1961 (d) 1965
25. Cutter's scheme of classification is known as:
    (a) Subject Classification
    (b) Expansive Classification
    (c) International Classification
    (d) BSO
26. Who is the first scholar of Book Classification?
    (a) Gesner (b) Dewey
    (c) Bacon (d) Cutter
27. 'Prolegomena' is related to:
    (a) Classification (b) Management
    (c) Cataloguing (d) Documentation
28. Who is the author of "Library Book Selection":
    (a) S. R. Ranganathan (b) C. A. Cutter
    (c) M. Dewey (d) J. D. Brown
29. The author of 'Classification and Communication' is:
    (a) Dr. Ranganathan (b) H. E. Bliss
    (c) M. Dewey (d) W. C. B. Sayers
30. The author of the book 'Elements of Library Classification' is:
    (a) S. R. Ranganathan (b) J. D. Brown
    (c) Fermont Rider (d) C. A. Cutter
31. Who is the author of 'Library Classification: Fundamentals and procedure':
    (a) Sayers (b) Bliss
    (c) Cutter (d) Ranganathan

Ans. : 24. (a) 25. (b) 26. (c) 27. (a) 28. (a) 29. (a) 30. (a) 31. (d)

32. Bibliographic Classification was devised by:
    (a) J. D. Brown (b) H. E. Bliss
    (c) C. A. Cutter (d) F. Rider

33. The third International Study Conference on Classification Research was held at:
    (a) London (b) New York
    (c) Paris (d) Mumbai

34. Auto abstract is based on the idea given by:
    (a) Derek Austin (b) B. C. Vickery
    (c) H. P. Luhn (d) F. W. Lancaster

35. British Museum Code was formulated by:
    (a) Bliss (b) Brown
    (c) Panizzi (d) Sayers

36. Benjamin A. Custer edited:
    (a) AACR - II (b) LISA
    (c) ILSA (d) 19th edition of DDC

37. Abridged edition of UDC is available in how many languages:
    (a) 7 (b) 12
    (c) 17 (d) 22

38. Basic structure of main classes in UDC is based on DDC.
    (a) True (b) False

39. Who enumerated the three postulates of Knowledge Classification i.e. idea plane, verbal plane, and rotational plane:
    (a) Margaret Mann (b) C. A. Cutter
    (c) W. C. B. Sayers (d) S. R. Ranganathan

Ans. : 32. (b) 33. (d) 34. (c) 35. (c) 36. (d) 37. (c) 38. (a) 39. (d)

40. The author of the book 'Classification and International Documentation' is:
    (a) S. R. Ranganathan (b) W. C. B. Sayers
    (c) Margaret Mann (d) J. S. Mills

41. Detailed classification required for micro documents is known as:
    (a) Library Classification
    (b) Broad Classification
    (c) Depth Classification
    (d) Bibliographic Classification

42. Library of Congress classification scheme is based upon:
    (a) Collocation (b) Users warrant
    (c) Literary warrant (d) APUPA pattern

43. The 2nd edition of bibliographic classification is known as BC-2 prepared in U.K. and devised by:
    (a) H. E. Bliss (b) J. Mills
    (c) G. A. Leoyd (d) Eric J. Coates

44. Subject Classification of J. D. Brown is an example of .... Classification:
    (a) Enumerative (b) Faceted
    (c) Freely faceted (d) Almost enumerative

45. In which classification scheme the first relation sign double colon (: :) is used when a reversai of two facets is not required:
    (a) CC (b) LC
    (c) DDC (d) UDC

Ans. : 40. (a) 41. (c) 42. (c) 43. (b) 44. (d) 45. (d)

46. A traditional subdivision of an old main class is known as .... classification:

    (a) Canonical (b) Specials main

    (c) Systems main (d) All of the above

47. Dr. Ranganathan formulated 43 canons of classification and grouped then into .... planes of work:

    (a) Two (b) Three

    (c) Four (d) Six

48. Universal Decimal Classification is:

    (a) Faceted classification

    (b) Fully faceted classification

    (c) Enumerative classification

    (d) None of the above

49. The real meaning of philosophical classification is based on:

    (a) Philosophy (b) Philosophy and Logic

    (c) Psychology (d) None of the above

50. In DDC, table 5 is for:

    (a) Area

    (b) Language

    (c) Persons

    (d) Racial, Ethnic, National Groups

51. In UDC, symbol (+) is used for:

    (a) And (b) Or

    (c) Relation (d) Extension

Ans. : 46. (a) 47. (b) 48. (c) 49. (b) 50. (d) 51. (a)

52. In DDC, table of precedence are provided so that three can be:
    (a) Addition of standard subdivision
    (b) Alternative ways of arrangement
    (c) Consistency
    (d) None of the above
53. DDC was first published in two volumes in the year:
    (a) 1956 (b) 1958
    (c) 1959 (d) 1963
54. According to C.C., the title 'Statistic for lawyers' is an example of:
    (a) Inter-array phase relationship
    (b) Inter-facet phase relationship
    (c) Inter-subject phase relationship
    (d) None of these
55. Interaction between two facets is called:
    (a) Intra array (b) Intra facet
    (c) Intra subject (d) None of the above
56. Naturopathy, Homeopathy and Ayurveda in Medicine class of C.C. are:
    (a) Specials (b) Systems
    (c) Both 'a' and 'b' (d) None
57. Who is not related to 7th edition of C.C.:
    (a) Gopinath (b) Neelameghan
    (c) Seetharama (d) All the above
58. Under main class Biology (G) of Colon Classification [M] is:
    (a) Organ Facet (b) Solution Facet
    (c) Substance Facet (d) Problem Facet

Ans. : 52. (c) 53. (b) 54. (c) 55. (b) 56. (b) 57. (a) 58. (c)

59. Who is the publisher of 1st edition of C.C.:
    (a) Indica Publication
    (b) Asia Publishing House
    (c) DRTC
    (d) INSDOC

60. The publisher of 7th edition of C.C.:
    (a) Sharda Ranganathan Endswement
    (b) Asia Publishing House
    (c) DTRC
    (d) Indian Bibliographies Bureau

61. The central core of a subject in C.C. is:
    (a) Personality (b) Matter
    (c) Energy (d) Time

62. 'Notation as a short hand sign' said by:
    (a) Ranganathan (b) Richardson
    (c) M. Mann (d) Sayers

63. 'Retroactive ordinal notation' was invented by:
    (a) J. S. Mills (b) J. D. Brown
    (c) Foskett (d) E. J. Coasts

64. 'Use of 1, 2, 3.............9 and A, B, C................. Z is an example of:
    (a) Pure Notation (b) Mixed Notation
    (c) Both (d) None of these

65. In which year Dr. Ranganathan was enunciated design of depth classification methodology:
    (a) 1964 (b) 1965
    (c) 1966 (d) 1967

Ans. : 59. (b) 60. (c) 61. (a) 62. (c) 63. (d) 64. (b) 65. (a)

66. Match the following:

(1) Biology	(a) I
(2) Botany	(b) K
(3) Zoology	(c) G
(4) Fine Arts	(d) N

Answers:

(a) 1 (a), 2 (b), 3 (c), 4 (d)

(b) 1 (a), 2 (c), 3 (b), 4 (d)

(c) 1 (c), 2 (b), 3 (a), 4 (d)

(d) 1 (c), 2 (a), 3 (b), 4 (d)

67. Three types of the fundamental category matter [M] as introduced in Colon Classification - 7th edition is:

(a) Material, method, property

(b) Material, method, utility

(c) Method, property, utility

(d) None of the above

68. Canon of Terminology is a canon for Verbal Plane:

(a) True (b) False

69. Mapping subjects in DDC proceeds from general to particular and end up with hierarchical chains:

(a) True (b) False

70. Universal Decimal Classification was propounded by Henry La Fontaine and Paul Otlet.

(a) True (b) False

71. DRTC is promoting research in the field of:

(a) Library Cataloguing (b) Library Management

(c) Library Classification (d) None of the above

Ans. : 66. (d) 67. (b) 68. (a) 69. (a)
70. (a) 71. (c)

72. In Colon Classification, in main class Z (Law), the class number for [E] is obtained by:

(a) Subject device (b) Geographical device

(c) Both (d) None of these

73. The ordinal value of the digit HZ (Mining) lies between:

(a) E and F (b) G and H

(c) H and I (d) I and J

74. The ordinal value of the digit LZ (Pharmacognosy) lies between (according to CC):

(a) K and L (b) L and M

(c) KZ and L (d) M and N

75. The table of standard subdivision helps a classification scheme:

(a) To add mnemonic value

(b) To ensure consistency

(c) Both 'a' and 'b'

(d) None of the above

76. In DDC phoenix schedules represent:

(a) Classes which are completely changed

(b) Classes which are slightly modified

(c) Classes to be modified in the future

(d) Classes not to be modified

77. Phoenix schedules are part of UDC.

(a) True (b) False

78. In UDC the symbol -03 (hyphen naught three) denotes the common auxiliaries of:

(a) Form (b) Place

(c) Person (d) Materials

Ans. : 72. (c) 73. (c) 74. (b) 75. (c) 76. (a) 77. (b) 78. (c)

79. In Colon Classification, digit 3 in space isolate stands for:
    (a) Mother country (b) Favoured country
    (c) Muslim country (d) Asia

80. PMEST order is applied with in:
    (a) Basic classes (b) Canonical classes
    (c) Main classes (d) None of these

81. Phase relations may have to be shown at the:
    (a) Array level (b) Facet level
    (c) Subject level (d) All of the above

82. Colon Classification was first published in the year 1933.
    (a) True (b) False

83. Which phase relation is not provided in CC–61st edition:
    (a) Difference (b) Influencing
    (c) Tool (d) Bias

84. Who was the author of 'Heading and Canons':
    (a) M. Mann (b) Dr. Ranganathan
    (c) E. J. Coats (d) C. A. Cutter

85. The author of the book 'Theory of Library Catalogue' is:
    (a) J. D. Brown (b) Charles Ammi Cutter
    (c) W. C. B. Sayers (d) S. R. Ranganathan

86. 'International Cataloguing' is a quarterly bulletin of:
    (a) ILA (b) ALA
    (c) IFLA (d) FID

87. Cutter's rules for dictionary catalogue' are devised by C. A. Cutter, first published in 1876.
    (a) True (b) False

Ans. :	79. (b)	80. (c)	81. (d)	82. (a)
	83. (c)	84. (b)	85. (d)	86. (c)
	87. (a)			

88. The card catalogue was first introduced in France in the year:

(a) 1757 (b) 1791

(c) 1857 (d) 1891

89. International Conference on Cataloguing Principles (ICCP) was held at Paris in:

(a) 1952 (b) 1955

(c) 1961 (d) 1965

90. Which is not the inner form of catalogue:

(a) Card form of the catalogue

(b) Dictionary catalogue

(c) Classified catalogue

(d) All of the above

91. Canon of Recall Value was introduced by:

(a) Ranganathan (b) Cutter

(c) Coats (d) C. Bhattacharya

92. Canon of Recall Value relates to the rendering of:

(a) Class Number (b) Tracing

(c) Notes (d) Heading

93. Cataloguing in Publication Programme was introduced by:

(a) British Library

(b) Library of Congress

(c) Indian Library Association

(d) IFLA

94. 'Pre-natal Cataloguing' is a contribution of:

(a) ILA (b) ALA

(c) Library of Congress (d) Dr. Ranganathan

Ans. : 88. (b) 89. (c) 90. (a) 91. (a) 92. (d) 93. (b) 94. (d)

95. Library catalogue helps to bring all resources on a particular on a particular subject together which are scattered throughout the collection.
    (a) True (b) False

96. Match the following:

(1) CIP Programme	(a) 1743
(2) CIS Programme	(b) 1958
(3) ICCP	(c) 1971
(4) Card catalogue	(d) 1961

    Answers:
    (a) 1 (a), 2 (b), 3 (c), 4 (d)
    (b) 1 (b), 2 (a), 3 (d), 4 (c)
    (c) 1 (c), 2 (b), 3 (d), 4 (a)
    (d) 1 (b), 2 (c), 3 (a), 4 (d)

97. Canon of Sought Heading related to:
    (a) Classification (b) Cataloguing
    (c) Management (d) Reference service

98. Analytical entry is prepared for:
    (a) Full document
    (b) Translated document
    (c) Alternative title
    (d) Part of a document

99. Which of the following term was first used by Ranganathan:
    (a) Cataloguing in Source
    (b) Cataloguing in Publication
    (c) Library Economy
    (d) None of the above

Ans. : 95. (a) 96. (c) 97. (b) 98. (d) 99. (d)

100. Match the following:

(1) Vatican Code	(a) 1908
(2) Anglo-American Code	(b) 1931
(3) Classified Catalogue Code	(c) 1934
(4) AACR - I	(d) 1967

Answers:

(a) 1 (a), 2 (b), 3 (c), 4 (d)
(b) 1 (a), 2 (c), 3 (d), 4 (b)
(c) 1 (b), 2 (c), 3 (d), 4 (a)
(d) 1 (b), 2 (a), 3 (c), 4 (d)

101. AACR - 2 was first published in 1978.
(a) True (b) False

102. In which year the Library of Congress was established:
(a) 1757 (b) 1800
(c) 1818 (d) 1857

103. Classified Catalogue is called by which name:
(a) Subject catalogue
(b) Author catalogue
(c) Title catalogue
(d) Alphabetical-Classed catalogue

104. 'Catalogue is a list of books, which is arranged on same define plan' - who define this:
(a) S. R. Ranganathan (b) J. D. Brown
(c) C. A. Cutter (d) Margaret Mann

105. Who is the co-author of the book 'Classified Catalogue Code' 5th edition with original author Dr. S. R. Ranganathan:
(a) M. A. Gopinath (b) A. Neelameghan
(c) Ganesh Bhattacharya (d) C. Bhattacharya

Ans. : 100. (d) 101. (a) 102. (b) 103. (a) 104. (c) 105. (b)

106. Which of the following canons of cataloguing is latest one propounded by S. R. Ranganathan:
    (a) Canon of Sought Heading
    (b) Canon of Prepotence
    (c) Canon of Recall Value
    (d) Canon of Ascertainability
107. The mixed catalogue of many libraries is known as:
    (a) Combined catalogue
    (b) Union catalogue
    (c) Joint catalogue
    (d) Co-operative catalogue
108. Machine Readable Catalogue (MARC) was started in which year:
    (a) 1965
    (b) 1966
    (c) 1967
    (d) 1968
109. Which of the following canon is related with the arrangement of entries:
    (a) Canon of recall value
    (b) Canon of Permanence
    (c) Canon of Sought Heading
    (d) Canon of Prepotence
110. Match the following:

(1) Anglo-American code	(a) W.W.Wishop and J.C.M.Hanson
(2) AACR-2	(b) P.W.Winter and M. Gorman
(3) Vatican Code	(c) LA (UK) and ALA

Answers:
    (a) 1 (a), 2 (b), 3 (c)
    (b) 1 (b), 2 (a), 3 (c)
    (c) 1 (c), 2 (b), 3 (a)
    (d) None of the above

Ans. : 106. (c) 107. (b) 108. (b) 109. (d) 110. (c)

111. Classified catalogue code was designed by:
   (a) C. A. Cutter (b) M. A. Gopinath
   (c) C. Bhattacharya (d) None of the above

112. Which of the following is Number Entry in Classified Catalogue Code:
   (a) CIE (b) BIE
   (c) CRE (d) CRIE

113. The left hand area of the Tracing Section in C.C.C. is used for:
   (a) CRE (b) CIE
   (c) BIE (d) CRIE

114. In Classified Catalogue Code 'Pseudonym - Real Name Entry' is a:
   (a) Class Reference Entry (b) Class Index /Entry
   (c) Book Index Entry
   (d) Cross Reference Index Entry

115. In C.C.C., Book Index Entry is prepared for:
   (a) Author (b) Editor
   (c) Fanciful Title (d) All of the above

116. The first rules for subject cataloguing was formalized by:
   (a) D. M. Norris
   (b) C. A. Cutter
   (c) S. R. Ranganathan
   (d) Library Association (U.K.)

117. Which popular, but complicated code was published in 1949:
   (a) LC Code (b) BM Code
   (c) ALA Code (d) AA Code

Ans. : 111. (d) 112. (c) 113. (b) 114. (d)
115. (d) 116. (b) 117. (c)

118. In the context of AACR - I, which of the following was not associated with:
    (a) Library Association (UK)
    (b) American Library Association
    (c) Canadian Library Association
    (d) UPLA
119. Sub-title in AACR - 2 is preceded by a colon symbol.
    (a) True (b) False
120. The code that recognizes the concept of 'Principal Author' is:
    (a) Vatican Code
    (b) AACR - I
    (c) ALA Code
    (d) Classified Catalogue Code
121. Indicator symbol for statement of responsibility in AACR - 2 is:
    (a) Colon (b) Semicolon
    (c) Hyphen (d) Diagonal slash
122. In AACR - 2 heading of corporate authorship are separated by full stop symbol.
    (a) True (b) False
123. The Chain Procedure was introduced in 1938 by S. R. Ranganathan.
    (a) True (b) False
124. Dr. Ranganathan's chain procedure is meant for:
    (a) Classification
    (b) Cataloguing
    (c) Deriving Subject Heading
    (d) None of these

Ans. : 118. (d) 119. (a) 120. (b) 121. (d)
122. (a) 123. (a) 124. (c)

125. Name Catalogue is variant form of:
    (a) Author catalogue (b) Subject catalogue
    (c) Title catalogue (d) All of the above
126. Canon of Currency is the canon of:
    (a) Notational plane (b) Verbal plane
    (c) Idea plane (d) None of the above
127. Which of the following is Number Entry in C.C.C.:
    (a) CIE (b) BIE
    (c) CRE (d) CRIE
128. Class Index Entries are derived from Class Number.
    (a) True (b) False
129. Classified Catalogue Code is mainly divided into 3 parts and AACR - 2 is divided into 2 parts.
    (a) True (b) False
130. How many rules are there under the heading 'Choice of Number' about Pseudonym according to AACR -2:
    (a) 19 (b) 22
    (c) 35 (d) 47
131. Indicator digit in AACR - 2 to join two parallel titles is:
    (a) Stroke (/) (b) Hyphen (-)
    (c) Equal Sign (=) (d) Semicolon (;)
132. In AACR - 2, the connecting symbol used between place of publisher and name of publisher is:
    (a) Semicolon (;) (b) Hyphen (-)
    (c) Comma (,) (d) Colon (:)
133. Dictionary Catalogue is more useful in:
    (a) Public Library (b) Academic Library
    (c) Research Library (d) All of the above

Ans. : **125. (a) 126. (b) 127. (c) 128. (a) 129. (a) 130. (a) 131. (c) 132. (d) 133. (a)**

134. Abbreviation OPEC stands for:
   (a) Ohio Public Access Cataloguing
   (b) On-line Public Access Catalogue
   (c) On-line Ohio Public Access Catalogue
   (d) None of these

135. Which one is not Pseudonym in the following:
   (a) Premchand (b) Nirala
   (c) Kabir (d) Ageya

136. Which one is Pseudonym in the following:
   (a) Kabir (b) Nirala
   (c) Jai Shankar Prasad (d) Mira

137. According to CCC, the rendering of the name A. P. Gathar will be as:
   (a) A. P. Gathar (b) Gathar, A. P.
   (c) GATHAR (A. P.) (d) Gather (À. P.)

138. The concept of Library - hand is given in:
   (a) AACR - 2
   (b) LC Catalogue code
   (c) Cutter's Rules for Dictionary Catalogue
   (d) Classified Catalogue Code

139. AACR -2 provides rules for descriptive cataloguing and choice of entry heading:
   (a) True (b) False

140. Which of the following catalogue code is based in ICCP:
   (a) CCC
   (b) Vatican Code
   (c) AACR - I
   (d) Rules for Dictionary Catalogue

Ans. : 134. (b) 135. (c) 136. (b) 137. (c) 138. (d) 139. (a) 140. (c)

141. In 6th edition of C.C., Common isolates are of two types namely:

(a) General and Special

(b) ACI and PCI

(c) Time CI and Space CI

(d) Energy CI and Time CI

142. According To CCC, the name of the president of India A. P. J. Abdul Kalam should be rendered as:

(a) India, President (Kalam, A P J Abdul)

(b) India, President (2002- : A P J Abdul Kalam)

(c) INDIA, PRESIDENT (A P J Abdul Kalam)

(d) Kalam, A P J Abdul (President : India : 2002)

143. Four groups given below, which one contains specific entries:

(a) CIE and CRIE (b) CRE and CRIE

(c) CRE and CIE (d) BIE and CRIE

144. Canon of Currency is the canon of:

(a) Idea plane (b) Verbal plane

(c) Notational plane (d) None of the above

145. Canon of Characteristic is a canon for:

(a) Idea plane (b) Verbal plane

(c) Notational plane (d) None of the above

146. In AACR -2 for serial publication, total number of volumes available in library are mentioned under:

(a) Title Section (b) Tracing Section

(c) Note Section (d) Collation Section

Ans. : 141. (b) 142. (b) 143. (d) 144. (b)
145. (a) 146. (d)

147. The provision in AACR -2 enter a pseudonymous author under his/her popular name, even if it does not appear on title page, is violation of:
   (a) Canon of Recall Value
   (b) Canon of Prepotence
   (c) Canon of Currency
   (d) Canon of Ascertainability

148. According to AACR - 2, University Grants Commission (India) will be rendered as:
   (a) India, University (Grants Commission)
   (b) India, Ministry of Education, University Grants Commission
   (c) India, University Grants Commission
   (d) University Grants Commission, India

149. The method of mapping of subjects in colon classification is:
   (a) Flexible (b) Hierarchical
   (c) Enumerative (d) Rigid

150. Match the following:

(1) H. E. Bliss	(a) 1892
(2) J. D. Brown	(b) 1870
(3) S. R .Ranganathan	(c) 1862

   Answers:
   (a) 1 (a), 2 (b), 3 (c)
   (b) 1 (b), 2 (c), 3 (a)
   (c) 1 (c), 2 (a), 3 (b)
   (d) 1 (a), 2 (c), 3 (b)

Ans. : 147. (d) 148. (b) 149. (a) 150. (b)

151. Match the following:

(1) BSO	(a) 1905
(2) UDC	(b) 1978
(3) DDC	(c) 1876
(4) CC	(d) 1933

Answers:

(a) 1 (a), 2 (b), 3 (c), 4 (d)
(b) 1 (a), 2 (c), 3 (b), 4 (d)
(c) 1 (b), 2 (d), 3 (a), 4 (c)
(d) 1 (b), 2 (a), 3 (c), 4 (d)

152. Colon Classification used Arabic numerals for recently recognized main classes in:

(a) First Zone (b) Second Zone
(c) Third Zone (d) Fifth Zone

153. According to AACR - II, Bible comes under the category of a/an:

(a) Uniform title
(b) Anonymous work
(c) Heavenly work
(d) Corporate authorship

154. In AACR - II, standard number ISSN is written:

(a) After physical description area
(b) After note area
(c) After tracing area
(d) In tracing area

155. As per CCC, the heading in the Class Index Entry are to be written in capitals form the first vertical.

(a) True (b) False

Ans. : 151. (d) 152. (b) 153. (a) 154. (b) 155. (a)

156. If all the volumes of the book, which have been published are not possessed by the library is called:
   (a) Half Set (b) Complete set
   (c) Incomplete set (d) Broken set
157. The subject 'General' falls under which main class of DDC:
   (a) 900 (b) 920
   (c) 910 (d) 930
158. Placing closely related subjects in close proximity in a scheme of classification is called:
   (a) Facet Sequence (b) Literary Warrant
   (c) Reduction (d) Collocation
159. The basis for the formulation of Cutter's Book Number is:
   (a) Name of the author (b) Size of the book
   (c) Subject (d) Colour of the book
160. Maintenance and distribution of DDC is carried out by:
   (a) BIS (b) OCLC
   (c) BSI (d) ISO
161. NADC is related with Co-operation catalogue:
   (a) True (b) False
162. Bar code Technology is useful for:
   (a) Acquisition (b) Circulation
   (c) Stock Tracking (d) All of the above
163. RFID tag has the ability to store information relating to the specific item to which they are attached, rewrite again without any requirement for contact or line of sight.
   (a) True (b) False

Ans. : 156. (c) 157. (b) 158. (d) 159. (a) 160. (b) 161. (a) 162. (d) 163. (a)

164. The advantage of RFID systems is:
   (a) Rapid check-out/ check-in
   (b) Automated materials handling
   (c) High-speed inventorying
   (d) All the above

Ans. : 164. (d)

6

Information, Communication, Library and Society

1. What was the earlier name of National library of India?
   (a) Asiatic Society Library
   (b) The Royal Library
   (c) Calcutta Public Library
   (d) Imperial Library of Calcutta
2. The period of 4th Five year plan was:
   (a) 1962-69 (b) 1955-61
   (c) 1969-74 (d) 1974-79
3. Hyderabad Public Library Act was passed in:
   (a) 1952 (b) 1955
   (c) 1965 (d) 1967

Ans. : 1. (d) 2. (c) 3. (b)

4. Abbreviation MALA stands for:
   (a) Manipur Library Association
   (b) Maharashtra Library Association
   (c) Moscow Library Association
   (d) Madras Library Association

5. INSDOC was setup as a/an:
   (a) UNESCO - ICSU Project (b) UNISIST Pilot Project
   (c) UNESCO Pilot Project (d) CSIR Pilot Project

6. Finance of public library is provided by:
   (a) Government (b) State Government
   (c) Public (d) All of the above

7. Khuda Baksa Oriental Public Library is situated at:
   (a) Lucknow (b) Agra
   (c) Aligarh (d) Patna

8. Match the following:

(1) ILA	(a) 1933
(2) ALA	(b) 1877
(3) LA (UK)	(c) 1876
(4) IFLA	(d) 1927

   Answers:
   (a) 1 (a), 2 (b), 3 (c), 4 (d)
   (b) 1 (a), 2 (c), 3 (b), 4 (d)
   (c) 1 (a), 2 (b), 3 (d), 4 (c)
   (d) 1 (d), 2 (c), 3 (b), 4 (a)

9. Central Drug Research Institute Library is:
   (a) Public (b) Academic
   (c) Special (d) None of these

Ans. : 4. (d) 5. (c) 6. (a) 7. (d)
8. (b) 9. (c)

10. An oldest library science journal in India is:
    (a) ABGILA (b) Library Quarterly
    (c) Library and Librarian (d) Library Miscellany
11. 'Prolegomena to Library Classification' is written by:
    (a) S. R. Ranganathan (b) W. C. B. Sayers
    (c) J. D. Brown
    (d) Ganesh Bhattacharya
12. Who is the author of 'Documentation and its facets':
    (a) H. P. Luhn (b) Frank Shepard
    (c) S. R. Ranganathan (d) Allen Kant
13. 'Science and Technology: Introduction to the literature' is written by:
    (a) D. J. Foskett (b) S. R. Ranganathan
    (c) Grogen (d) M. Taube
14. Who is the author of 'Theory of Library Catalogue'?
    (a) P. N. Kaula (b) S. R. Ranganathan
    (c) A. Neelameghan (d) M. A. Gopinath
15. Who was the publisher of ABGILA?
    (a) INSDOC
    (b) Indian Library Association
    (c) IASLIC
    (d) GILA
16. ABGILA was first published in:
    (a) 1949 (b) 1954
    (c) 1957 (d) 1964
17. The year of discontinued ABGILA was:
    (a) 1949 (b) 1957
    (c) 1958 (d) 1963

Ans. : 10. (d) 11. (a) 12. (c) 13. (c)
14. (b) 15. (b) 16. (a) 17. (c)

18. Match the following:

(1) GILA	(a) Nigeria
(2) IASLIC	(b) Kolkata
(3) GLA	(c) Shimla
(4) COMLA	(d) Guwahati

Answers:

(a) 1 (b), 2 (a), 3 (d), 4 (c)

(b) 1 (a), 2 (b), 3 (c), 4 (d)

(c) 1 (c), 2 (b), 3 (a), 4 (d)

(d) 1 (c), 2 (b), 3 (d), 4 (a)

19. What does GLA stands for:

(a) Guwahati Library Association

(b) Goa Library Association

(c) Gujarat Library Association

(d) None of these

20. The famous book 'Theory of Library Catalogue' was published in the year:

(a) 1936 (b) 1938

(c) 1940 (d) 1944

21. A.A.A. Fyzee was chairman of a Library Committee set up for:

(a) Varanasi (b) Baroda

(c) Bombay (d) Bangalore

22. The state, which does have library legislation:

(a) Jammu & Kashmir (b) Bihar

(c) Punjab (d) Goa

Ans. : 18. (d) 19. (a) 20. (b) 21. (c) 22. (d)

23. Mark, which is not a depository library:
    (a) National Library, Kolkata
    (b) Bombay University Library
    (c) Asiatic Society Library
    (d) Connemara Public Library
24. The journal 'Library science with slant to documentation' is published by DRTC.
    (a) True (b) False
25. Abbreviation RLA stands for:
    (a) Research Library Association
    (b) Rampur Library Association
    (c) Rajasthan Library Association
    (d) Roorkee Library Association
26. Delhi Public Library was set up as a/an:
    (a) INSDOC Pilot Project
    (b) UNESCO Pilot Project
    (c) UNISIST Pilot project
    (d) ILA Project
27. 'Booklist' is a publication of:
    (a) ILA (b) SLA
    (c) LA (UK) (d) ALA
28. The biggest and busiest Public Library of Asia is:
    (a) Delhi Public Library
    (b) Public Library of Japan
    (c) Bombay Public Library
    (d) Khuda Baksa Oriental Public Library

Ans. : 23. (b) 24. (a) 25. (d) 26. (b) 27. (d) 28. (a)

29. Bibliotheque Nationale is a public library, located at Paris.

    (a) True (b) False

30. British Council Library is an example of:

    (a) Academic Library (b) Public Library
    (c) Special Library (d) National Library

31. Report is an example of:

    (a) Indexing device
    (b) Abstracting device
    (c) Formal communication
    (d) Informal communication

32. Record of daily works in the library is known as:

    (a) Staff Manual (b) Staff Check Book
    (c) Staff Details Register (d) Library Check Book

33. Which tool is used to support the book on shelves:

    (a) Book box (b) Book desk rod
    (c) Book tibox (d) Book supporter

34. By which section accession work of books is carried out:

    (a) Circulation Section (b) Reference Section
    (c) Administration Section (d) Acquisition Section

35. Size of Library Card is:

    (a) 12.5cm × 7.5cm (b) 12.7cm × 7.7cm
    (c) 12cm × 7cm (d) 5cm × 3cm

Ans. : 29. (a) 30. (b) 31. (c) 32. (a)
33. (d) 34. (d) 35. (a)

36. Match the following:

(1) ALA	(a) USA
(2) ILA	(b) India
(3) LA (UK)	(c) UK
(4) IFLA	(d) Niderland

Answers:

(a) 1 (a), 2 (b), 3 (c), 4 (d)

(b) 1 (a), 2 (b), 3 (c), 4 (c)

(c) 1 (c), 2 (b), 3 (a), 4 (d)

(d) 1 (b), 2 (a), 3 (c), 4 (d)

37. Indian Library Association (ILA) is a member of IFLA and COMLA.

(a) True (b) False

38. Public Law 480 (PL 480) is an American law.

(a) True (b) False

39. Half leather is associated with:

(a) Binding (b) Budgeting

(c) Forecasting (d) All the above

40. Brown system is associated with:

(a) Book selection (b) Cataloguing

(c) Circulation (d) Serial Control

41. What is 'POSDCORB'?

(a) Pre capital method

(b) Principles of Scientific Management

(c) Foreign exchange rates

(d) System analysis

Ans. : 36. (a) 37. (a) 38. (a) 39. (a) 40. (c) 41. (b)

42. Paper editions are better and durable than library editions.

    (a) True (b) False

43. Which of the following is a pseudonym:

    (a) Jai Shankar Prasad
    (b) Kabir
    (c) Prenchand
    (d) Suryakant Tripathi 'Nirala'

44. Match the following:

    (1) ASLIB (a) 1933
    (2) IASLIC (b) 1924
    (3) COMLA (c) 1955
    (4) GILA (d) 1972

    Answers:

    (a) 1 (b), 2 (c), 3 (a), 4 (d)
    (b) 1 (b), 2 (c), 3 (d), 4 (a)
    (c) 1 (d), 2 (c), 3 (a), 4 (b)
    (d) 1 (d), 2 (c), 3 (b), 4 (a)

45. 'Preparatory Studies' and 'Fallow-up Studies' concept were given in the context of functions of University Library by:

    (a) Dr. S. R. Ranganthan (b) K. P. Shinha
    (c) B. S. Keshavan (d) U. G. C.

46. JOCLAI is the combination of ILA, IASLIC and IATLIS.

    (a) True (b) False

47. 'Thesaurus of English Words and Phrase' was first published in:

    (a) 1842 (b) 1852
    (c) 1857 (d) 1885

Ans. : 42. (a) 43. (c) 44. (b) 45. (a)
46. (a) 47. (b)

48. 'Thesaurus of English Words and Phrase' was presented by:
    (a) B. Dancer (b) J. Mills
    (c) J. M. Paterson (d) P. M. Rogel
49. TEST is an example of:
    (a) Thesaurus (b) Handbook
    (c) Text Book (d) Research report
50. Abbreviation TEST stands for:
    (a) Thesaurus of Scientific Test
    (b) Thesaurus of Science and Technology
    (c) Thesaurus of Electronic, Science & Technology
    (d) Thesaurus of Engineering and Scientific Test
51. TEST thesaurus was first published in the year:
    (a) 1964 (b) 1966
    (c) 1968 (d) 1972
52. INSPEC is a/an:
    (a) Handbook (b) New York
    (c) Thesaurus (d) Bibliography
53. The first step in the construction of thesaurus in:
    (a) Define the field area
    (b) Collection of terms
    (c) Subject Heading Categorization
    (d) Concept formation
54. NLM stands for:
    (a) National Library of Moreland
    (b) National Library of Medicine
    (c) National Medical Library
    (d) Moreland National Library

Ans. : 48. (d) 49. (a) 50. (d) 51. (a) 52. (c) 53. (a) 54. (b)

55. Match the following:

(1) RLA	(a) Rajasthan
(2) MALA	(b) Chennai
(3) COMLA	(c) The Hauge
(4) IFLA	(d) Nigeria

Answers:

(a) 1 (a), 2 (b), 3 (c), 4 (d)

(b) 1 (c), 2 (b), 3 (d), 4 (c)

(c) 1 (a), 2 (b), 3 (d), 4 (c)

(d) 1 (a), 2 (b), 3 (c), 4 (c)

56. Special Library Association (SLA), Association of Special Library (ASLIB) and IASLIC are related to:

(a) Public library (b) Academic library

(c) National library (d) Special library

57. Which of the following libraries do not received books under 'Delivery of Book Act':

(a) Delhi Public Library

(b) Connemara Public Library

(c) National Library, Kolkata

(d) Karmaicel Library

58. The first 'Model public libraries act' in India was drafted in the year:

(a) 1931 (b) 1942

(c) 1948 (d) 1949

Ans. : 55. (c) 56. (d) 57. (d) 58. (b)

59. Match the following:

(1)	Karnataka Public Libraries Act	(a)	1965
(2)	Manipur Public Libraries Act	(b)	1993
(3)	Pondicherry Public Libraries Act	(c)	1988
(4)	Goa Public Libraries Act	(d)	1994

Answers:

(a) 1 (a), 2 (c), 3 (b), 4 (d)
(b) 1 (a), 2 (b), 3 (c), 4 (d)
(c) 1 (a), 2 (c), 3 (d), 4 (b)
(d) 1 (a), 2 (d), 3 (b), 4 (c)

60. The first professional journal in Library Science is:
(a) ABGILA (b) LISA
(c) ILSA (d) Library journal

61. The first professional journal in Library Science was started in:
(a) 1757 (b) 1786
(c) 1876 (d) 1887

62. Match the following:

(1)	Choice	(a)	IFLA
(2)	International Cataloguing	(b)	IASLIC
(3)	ILSA	(c)	LA (UK)
(4)	Journal of Librarianship	(d)	ALA

Answers:

(a) 1 (a), 2 (d), 3 (b), 4 (c)
(b) 1 (b), 2 (b), 3 (b), 4 (a)
(c) 1 (c), 2 (a), 3 (b), 4 (d)
(d) 1 (d), 2 (a), 3 (b), 4 (c)

Ans. : 59. (a) 60. (b) 61. (c) 62. (d)

63. 'ALA list of Subject Heading for use in Dictionary Catalogue - 1st edition' was published in:

    (a) 1895 (b) 1899

    (c) 1904 (d) 1908

64. 'ALA list of Subject Heading for use in Dictionary Catalogue - 3rd edition' was published in the year:

    (a) 1909 (b) 1911

    (c) 1913 (d) 1915

65. 'ALA list of Subject Heading for use in Dictionary Catalogue of LC - 1st edition' was published in the year:

    (a) 1901-04 (b) 1910-14

    (c) 1911-15 (d) 1923-27

66. 'Sears List of Subject Headings' was first published in the year:

    (a) 1908 (b) 1911

    (c) 1917 (d) 1923

67. 'Sears List of Subject Headings - 14th edition' was published in the year:

    (a) 1972 (b) 1983

    (c) 1991 (d) 2001

68. Who is the publisher of 'A Subject Heading for Children Material'?

    (a) LA, London (b) ALA, Chichago

    (c) SLA, New York (d) None of these

69. 'A Subject Heading for Children Material' was first published in the year:

    (a) 1923 (b) 1951

    (c) 1978 (d) 1979

Ans. : 63. (a) 64. (b) 65. (b) 66. (d) 67. (c) 68. (b) 69. (b)

70. Match the following:

(1) SLA	(a) United Kingdom
(2) IASLIC	(b) India
(3) ASLIB	(c) United State

Answers:

(a) 1 (a), 2 (c), 3 (b) (b) 1 (a), 2 (b), 3 (c)
(c) 1 (a), 2 (b), 3 (a) (d) 1 (c), 2 (b), 3 (a)

71. Salarjung Museum Library is at:
(a) Bhopal (b) Hyderabad
(c) Lucknow (d) Patna

72. Who is the publisher of 'Eviation Subject Headings and Classification Guide':
(a) IASLIC, Kolkata
(b) Library Association (UK)
(c) American Library Association
(d) Special Library Association, New York

73. Abbreviation RRRLF stands for:
(a) Raja Rammohan Rai Library Foundation
(b) Rajasthan Research Library Foundation
(c) Raja Rammohan Rai Library Federation
(d) Rammohan Rai Research Library Foundation

74. Raja Rammohan Rai Library Foundation was set up in Kolkata (Calcutta) in:
(a) 1960 (b) 1962
(c) 1972 (d) 1973

75. What does BSO stand for:
(a) Broad Service of Ordering
(b) Broad System of Ordering
(c) British System of Ordering
(d) Bibliographical System of Ordering

Ans. : 70. (d) 71. (b) 72. (d) 73. (a) 74. (c) 75. (b)

76. Match the following:

(1) SLA	(a) 1924
(2) IASLIC	(b) 1909
(3) ASLIB	(c) 1955

Answers:

(a) 1 (a), 2 (b), 3 (c) (b) 1 (a), 2 (c), 3 (b)
(c) 1 (b), 2 (a), 3 (c) (d) 1 (c), 2 (a), 3 (b)

77. SRC (Subject Reference Code) is used in:
(a) BSO (b) CC
(c) AACR - 1 (d) AACR - 2

78. Goa Public Libraries Act was passed in:
(a) 1988 (b) 1989
(c) 1993 (d) 1994

79. Pondicherry Public Libraries Act was passed in the year:
(a) 1992 (b) 1993
(c) 1994 (d) 1996

80. The Madras Public Libraires Act provides for library cess to be levied by Local Government.
(a) True (b) False

81. Which of the following is an Indological Library:
(a) Delhi Public Library, Delhi
(b) Karmaicel Public Library, Varanasi
(c) National Library, Kolkata
(d) St. Xavier College Library, Mumbai

82. 'Library Association Record' is related to which of the following Library Association:
(a) ILA (b) ALA
(c) LA (d) SLA

Ans. : 76. (c) 77. (a) 78. (d) 79. (b)
80. (a) 81. (c) 82. (c)

83. 'Publicity of library services to convert non-reader into reader', this concept is related to:
    (a) Public Library (b) Academic Library
    (c) Special Library (d) National Library
84. Which of the following libraries is responsible to provide its services 'free of charge' without distinction of caste, creed or sex:
    (a) National library (b) Public library
    (c) University library (d) Special library
85. Conversation of Local History is the:
    (a) Main function of public library
    (b) One of the function of pubic library
    (c) Function of a school library
    (d) None of the above
86. Resource Sharing is not possible in area of:
    (a) Library function (b) Library services
    (c) Library users (d) None of these
87. Mark the odd (clue: Resource Sharing)
    (a) BIOSIS (b) RLIN
    (c) OCLC (d) INFLIBNET
88. Which of the following is not barrier in library resources sharing:
    (a) Inadequate library Collection
    (b) Revelries between parent bodies
    (c) Predetermined term and conditions
    (d) Cumbersome library procedures

Ans. : 83. (a) 84. (b) 85. (b) 86. (c)
87. (a) 88. (c)

89. What is not the constraint in resources sharing:
    (a) Custodian mentality of libraries
    (b) Inefficient means of communication
    (c) Leadership to initiate cooperative Ventures
    (d) Fear of loss

90. How the use of library can be maximized:
    (a) Application of computers
    (b) User Education
    (c) Through Reference Service
    d) CAS

91. 'Bottom Card' is prepared in :
    (a) Two card system (b) Three card system
    (c) Network system (d) Kardex system

92. In the context of public library, 'Orientation Programme' should be carried out:
    (a) Twice a year
    (b) Thrice a year
    (c) At the beginning of the year
    (d) Through out the year

93. What does CBI stand for (clue: Bibliography):
    (a) Cumulative Book Index
    (b) Current Bibliographical Index
    (c) Central Bibliographical Institute
    (d) Current Bibliography of India

94. Accession List South Asia is now changed to:
    (a) The South Asia Accession List
    (b) The South Asian Bibliography
    (c) The South Asian Bibliographer
    (d) None of the above

Ans. : 89. (d) 90. (b) 91. (d) 92. (d) 93. (a) 94. (c)

95. 'Gazette' gives information about:
   (a) Old records (b) History of places
   (c) Places to see (d) None of these
96. The 'Imperical Gazetteer of India' is published by:
   (a) H. W. Wilson, New York
   (b) Clarendon Press, Oxford
   (c) Europa Publications, London
   (d) Indian Bibliographies Bureau, New Delhi
97. 'Research in Progress Bulletin' is an example of:
   (a) CAS (b) SDI
   (c) Indexing Journal (d) Abstracting Journal
98. PAIS is an:
   (a) Account of current events
   (b) Annotated bibliography
   (c) Abstracting service in public affairs
   (d) Indexing service on public affairs
99. Abbreviation PAIS stands for:
   (a) Public Access Indexing Service
   (b) Present Answer Information System
   (c) Public Affairs Information Service Bulletin
   (d) Public Answer Interchange Service
100. Who is the publisher of Demography Year Book:
   (a) United Nations, New York
   (b) Central Statistical Organization
   (c) Bureau of Census, Washington
   (d) Microsoft

Ans. : 95. (d) 96. (b) 97. (a) 98. (d)
99. (c) 100. (a)

101. 'Role Indicators' are used in:
   (a) POPSI (b) PRECIS
   (c) KWIC (d) KWOC
102. The term NT, BT and RT are used in:
   (a) KWIC (b) POPSI
   (c) LCSH (d) PRECIS
103. Webster's Collegiate Thesaurus follows:
   (a) Logical arrangement
   (b) Annalistic arrangement
   (c) Classified arrangement
   (d) Alphabetical arrangement
104. The term SA (See Also) and UF (Used For) are used in:
   (a) LC (b) LCSH
   (c) Classification Scheme (d) None of the above
105. 'Library Bill of right' is first published by ALA in the year:
   (a) 1948 (b) 1950
   (c) 1951 (d) 1955
106. Information policy is a boon for the development of each nation and countries.
   (a) True (b) False
107. The term Communication comes from:
   (a) Greek (b) German
   (c) Latin (d) French
108. In the field of communication, which technology was the first invented:
   (a) Telegram (b) Telegraph
   (c) Telegraphy (d) Telepathy

Ans. :

101. (b)	102. (c)	103. (d)	104. (b)
105. (a)	106. (a)	107. (c)	108. (a)

109. Which one is the vital component in information communication chain:
    (a) Researcher
    (b) Teacher
    (c) Libraries & Information Centres
    (d) None of the above
110. Dr. Ranganathan was appointed honorary professor of Library Science in 1947 at:
    (a) Madras University
    (b) Banaras Hindu University
    (c) Bombay University
    (d) Delhi University
111. Dr. S. R. Ranganathan was appointed as National Research Professor of Library Science in:
    (a) 1962 (b) 1959
    (c) 1957 (d) 1952
112. Model Public Library Act was presented by Dr. S. R. Ranganathan in:
    (a) 1930 (b) 1942
    (c) 1948 (d) 1957
113. Dr. S. R. Ranganathan was appointed chairman of the U. G. C. Library Committee in the year:
    (a) 1957 (b) 1959
    (c) 1961 (d) 1963
114. Who did prepare 'Library development plan' for India:
    (a) Peter Lazer (b) V. K. R. V. Rao
    (c) Radhakrishanan (d) Ranganathan

Ans. : 109. (c) 110. (d) 111. (a) 112. (a)
113. (b) 114. (d)

115. Dr. S. R. Ranganathan was the first chairman of U. G. C., India.

(a) True (b) False

116. Match the following:

(1) Parry Committee	(a) Public Libraries
(2) Kenyon Committee	(b) M. Lib. I. Sc.
(3) Lal Committee	(c) Academic Libraries

Answers:

(a) 1 (a), 2 (b), 3 (c) (b) 1 (c), 2 (a), 3 (b)

(c) 1 (b), 2 (c), 3 (a) (d) 1 (c), 2 (b), 3 (a)

117. The famous book 'Headings and Canons' is written by:

(a) Dr. Ranganathan (b) C. A. Cutter

(c) M. Dewey (d) W. C. B. Sayers

118. The book 'Post war reconstruction of libraries in India' was written by:

(a) P. N. Kaula (b) Prof. Yashpal

(c) S. Radhakrishanan (d) Dr. Ranganathan

119. The term 'Paperless Society' was coined by:

(a) Ranganathan (b) Lancaster

(c) Bell (d) None of these

120. The term 'Library Science' was first used by:

(a) Lancaster (b) Ranganathan

(c) Bell (d) J. Mills

121. The concept of 'Library warrant' was originated by:

(a) W. Hulme (b) S. R. Ranganathan

(c) M. Dewey (d) J. D. Browne

Ans. : 115. (a) 116. (b) 117. (a) 118. (d) 119. (b) 120. (b) 121. (a)

122. The concept of 'Academic state of Knowledge' was proposed by:
(a) S. R. Ranganathan (b) Lancaster
(c) Plato (d) Belkin and Vickery

123. The concept of 'Self-renewal' was introduced by:
(a) Dr. Parry (b) Danton
(c) M. B. Line (d) Atkinson

124. GOC stands for:
(a) Good Offices Committee
(b) Goods Offices Communication
(c) Government Office Committee
(d) None of the above

125. The term 'Library Science' was coined by:
(a) M. Dewey (b) Ranganathan
(c) Farradane (d) Lancaster

126. 'Mobile Library' is a kind of:
(a) Digital Library (b) Small Library
(c) Extension Services (d) Independent Library

127. The Imperial Library was founded by:
(a) Lord Mountbatten (b) Lord Curzon
(c) Queen Elizabeth - I (d) H. Harold

128. Which of the following is the method for recording the receipt of periodical publications:
(a) Kardex (b) Two card system
(c) Three card system (d) All the above

129. 'Shelf List' is monthly useful in:
(a) Book selection (b) Classification
(c) Stock verification (d) Reservation work

Ans. : 122. (b) 123. (d) 124. (a) 125. (b) 126. (c) 127. (b) 128. (d) 129. (c)

130. 'The library will subscribe journals through an agent' this is a statement of:
    (a) Policy (b) Procedure
    (c) Mission (d) Objective

131. Budget is a:
    (a) Financial method (b) Mechanical device
    (c) Control device (d) Both 'a' and 'b'

132. Which of the Budgeting System is the most suitable for a universe library:
    (a) Lump sum budgeting (b) Formula budgeting
    (c) PPBS
    (d) Zero based budgeting

133. Which of the following methods of financial estimation is the most suitable for a university library:
    (a) Proportional method
    (b) Per capita method
    (c) Per capita and methods of details
    (d) Proportional with the combination of any one method

134. Zero based budgeting system was developed by Peter Phyor in:
    (a) 1970 (b) 1971
    (c) 1972 (d) 1973

135. 'External' and 'Internal' environment is considered at the time of:
    (a) Planning (b) Motivating
    (c) Budgeting (d) Staffing

136. The term planning of library building consists of:
    (a) The librarian (b) The architect
    (c) The library authority (d) All of above

Ans. : 130. (b) 131. (c) 132. (d) 133. (d)
134. (a) 135. (c) 136. (d)

137. Match the following:

(1) ZBB	(a) Budgeting System
(2) PPBS	(b) Peter Phyor
(3) Demand Theory	(c) Mc Colvin

Answers:

(a) 1 (a), 2 (b), 3 (c) (b) 1 (b), 2 (a), 3 (c)
(c) 1 (b), 2 (c), 3 (a) (d) 1 (c), 2 (b), 3 (a)

138. How many Indian state have passed library legislation:
(a) Nine (b) Ten
(c) Eleven (d) Thirteen

139. William Allenson Border was associated with Public Library movement in:
(a) Andhra Pradesh (b) Baroda
(c) Punjab (d) Maharashtra

140. A. D. Dickinson was associated with Public Library movement in:
(a) Andhra Pradesh (b) Baroda
(c) Punjab (d) Maharashtra

141. L. R. Fadneesh was associated with Public Library movement in:
(a) Delhi (b) Baroda
(c) Punjab (d) Maharashtra

142. 'Library is the heart of an institute', this was stated by:
(a) Dr. Radhakrishanan (b) Dr. Ranganathan
(c) V. K. R.V. Rao (d) B. S. Kesavan

143. ....celebrated as Librarian's day in India:
(a) 12th August (b) 30th September
(c) 14th November (d) 20th November

Ans. : **137. (b) 138. (d) 139. (b) 140. (c) 141. (d) 142. (a) 143. (a)**

144. How the use of library can be maximized:
    (a) Application of computers
    (b) Current Awareness Service
    (c) Through Reference Service
    (d) User Education

145. 'Initiation of freshman' is concerned with:
    (a) To provide reference service
    (b) To provide current awareness service
    (c) To intimate new user regarding library science
    (d) Introduction of library science to new users

146. 'Library quarterly' is published by:
    (a) University of Chicago (b) University of Illinois
    (c) B. H. U. (d) H. W. Wilson

147. 'Initiation Programme to New User', this term was coined by:
    (a) S. R. Ranganathan (b) Thomas G. Kirck
    (c) Patricia B. Knapp (d) Louis Shores

148. Library Orientation, user education, bibliography instruction are related in the following way:
    (a) All mean the same thing
    (b) Library orientation is wider and encompasses the other two
    (c) User education is wider and encompasses the other two
    (d) None of the above

149. 'College blue book' gives information on:
    (a) Courses of study in USA
    (b) List of colleges in USA
    (c) Scholarship and grants
    (d) All the above

Ans. : 144. (d) 145. (c) 146. (a) 147. (a) 148. (c) 149. (d)

150. Demographic Year Book is an annual publication of:
   (a) Central Statistical Organization
   (b) Statistical Office, London
   (c) United Nations, New York
   (d) Bureau of Census, Washington

151. 'Two Factor Theory' is introduced by:
   (a) Mc Gregor
   (b) A. Maslow
   (c) Peter Drucker
   (d) Dr. Fredrick Herzberg

152. Who gave this Slogan, 'Best books for the largest numbers at lest cost':
   (a) Melvil Dewey (b) C. A. Cutter
   (c) J. F. K. Drury (d) S. R. Ranganathan

153. Radhakrishanan commission was recommended that 6.5% of the University's Budget would be a reasonable expenditure on library.
   (a) True (b) False

154. The U. G. C. Library committee recommended that university provide Rs 20 per student and Rs 100 per teacher for acquiring reading material for its library.
   (a) True (b) False

155. Browne charging system originated from:
   (a) India (b) United Kingdom
   (c) United States (d) Brazil

156. The functional element of management are Planning, Organizing, Staffing, Directing, Coordinating, Reporting and Budgeting.
   (a) True (b) False

Ans. : 150. (c) 151. (d) 152. (a) 153. (a)
154. (a) 155. (c) 156. (a)

157. First Library Science course at university level started in India in:

(a) Delhi (b) Bombay

(c) Banaras (d) Chennai

158. Second Library Science course at university level was started in India in:

(a) Delhi (b) Bombay

(c) Banaras (d) Madras

159. Match the following:

(1) British Museum Act (a) 1972

(2) British Library Act (b) 1759

(3) Imperial Library Act (c) 1902

Answers:

(a) 1 (a), 2 (b), 3 (c) (b) 1 (a), 2 (c), 3 (b)

(c) 1 (b), 2 (a), 3 (c) (d) 1 (b), 2 (c), 3 (a)

160. Which of the following college experimental user education for first time:

(a) University of Chicago (b) Montieth College

(c) University of Bombay (d) Oxford University

161. Government of India Libraries Association (GILA) was formed in:

(a) Baroda (b) Roorkee

(c) Jaipur (d) Shimla

162. Library Week is organized in India every year during:

(a) 12 - 18 August (b) 14 - 20 September

(c) 10 - 16 November (d) 14 - 20 November

Ans. : 157. (d) 158. (c) 159. (c) 160. (b) 161. (d) 162. (d)

163. National Medical Library comes under:
   (a) Ministry of Health Services
   (b) Human resource Development
   (c) All India Institute of Medical Sciences
   (d) Maulana Azad Medical College

164. Who was the first Libraries to use the phrase 'Reference Interview':
   (a) James I. Wyre (b) Margaret Hutchins
   (c) Richard J. Beeler (d) Samuel Rothstein

165. Word 'Censorship' derived from:
   (a) Freench (b) Greek
   (c) Latin (d) None of these

166. 'Royal Asiatic Society' library was set up at Mumbai in:
   (a) 1804 (b) 1814
   (c) 1824 (d) 1854

167. Connemara Public Library was set up at Madras in the year:
   (a) 1850 (b) 1857
   (c) 1860 (d) 1867

168. Imperial Library was set up at Calcutta in the year:
   (a) 1882 (b) 1891
   (c) 1896 (d) 1902

169. 48th All India Library Conference is organized by Indian Library Association (ILA) in the year:
   (a) January. 2001 (b) January, 2002
   (c) January, 2003 (d) June, 2003

170. The Term 'Slant in Abstract' was used by:
   (a) M. Taube (b) B. Guha
   (c) Dr. Ranganathan (d) J. H. Shera

Ans. :

163. (a)	164. (b)	165. (c)	166. (a)
167. (c)	168. (b)	169. (c)	170. (c)

171. 49th All India Library Conference is organized by ILA and hosted at:
    (a) University of Pune
    (b) SNDT Women's College
    (c) Banaras Hindu University
    (d) Bundelkhand University, Jhansi

172. Source, Channel and Recipient are the components of:
    (a) Information
    (b) Communication
    (c) Indexing
    (d) Problems theory of information

173. Semantic theory of information is referred to:
    (a) Shannon (b) Shannon & Weaver
    (c) J. H. Shera (d) Fairthorne

174. Indian Patents Office is located in:
    (a) New Delhi (b) Kolkata
    (c) Mumbai (d) Chennai

175. ILA was set up in 1933 under:
    (a) Societies Registration Act, 1857
    (b) Societies Registration Act, 1860
    (c) Societies Registration Act, 1885
    (d) Societies Registration Act, 1920

176. Abbreviation APALA stands for:
    (a) Asian Project and American Libraries Association
    (b) Asian Libraries Association - A Project
    (c) Asian Pacific American Libraries Association
    (d) None of these

Ans. : 171. (d) 172. (b) 173. (d) 174. (b) 175. (b) 176. (c)

177. Browne Charging system originated from:
   (a) USA (b) UK
   (c) Japan (d) South Africa

178. Which of the below named viceroy was associated with the enactment of 'Imperial Library Act':
   (a) Lord Minto (b) Lord Mount Batten
   (c) Lord Willington (d) Lord Curzon

179. Name of the Chairman of National Library Review Committee (1967) is:
   (a) S. R. Ranganathan (b) K. P. Shinha
   (c) V. S. Jha (d) V. K. R. V. Rao

180. The headquarter of Uttar Pradesh Library Association (UPLA) is situated in:
   (a) Kanpur (b) Lucknow
   (c) Agra (d) Allahabad

181. Central Drug Research Institute Library is a kind of:
   (a) Public Library (b) Academic Library
   (c) Special Library (d) Others

182. NATIS project was sponsored by:
   (a) IFLA (b) FID
   (c) UNESCO (d) SENDOC

183. National Information Centre for Textiles and Allied Subjects (NICTAS) was established in 1986 at:
   (a) New Delhi (b) Bengaluru
   (c) Lucknow (d) Ahmedabad

184. 'Every book its reader' is......................law of library science
   (a) Second (b) Third
   (c) Fourth (d) Fifth

Ans. :

177. (a)	178 (d)	179. (c)	180. (b)
181. (c)	182. (c)	183. (d)	184. (b)

185. Information policy for socio-economic development was initiated in 1979 by:
(a) NISSAT (b) UNIDO
(c) UNESCO (d) UNISEF

186. Information Economy includes within its preview:
(a) Information machinery
(b) Information work force
(c) Both 'a' and 'b'
(d) None of these

187. Credit goes to adopting scientific policy resolution to:
(a) Dr. Radhakrishanan
(b) Santi Swarup Bhatnagar
(c) Aurobindo
(d) Jawaharlal Nehru

188. Three levels of communication problems were defined by:
(a) Shannon (b) Bell
(c) Weaver (d) Shera

189. 'Library Technology Reports' is a publication of:
(a) ILA (b) LA (UK)
(c) ALA (d) UPLA

190. "Library Science with a slant to Documentation' is published by:
(a) IASLIC (b) DRTC
(c) ILA (d) RRRLF

191. 'Granthana' is a publication of:
(a) RRRLF (b) IASLIC
(c) IATLIS (d) GILA

Ans. :

185. (c)	186. (c)	187. (d)	188. (c)
189. (c)	190. (b)	191. (a)	

192. Dr. S. R. Ranganathan was the first chairman of U. G. C. (India).
   (a) True (b) False
193. V. K. R. V. Rao was the chairman of the working group on libraries (1964), set up by Planning Commission.
   (a) True (b) False
194. 'Library Bill of right' is a publication of:
   (a) LA (UK) (b) ALA
   (c) SLA (d) ILA
195. Melvil Dewey is known as father of library movement of USA.
   (a) True (b) False
196. Tata consultancy library falls under the category of:
   (a) Public library (b) Office library
   (c) Special library (d) All of the above
197. Which one of the following types of libraries has a variety of library clientele.
   (a) Public library (b) School library
   (c) Special library (d) Academic library
198. The original concept of 'Library Cooperation' is traced to:
   (a) OCLC (b) Dealer library plan
   (c) Both 'a' and 'b' (d) None of the above
199. The India input centre for INIS is:
   (a) IISC (b) TIFR
   (c) BARC (d) All of the above
200. The resource sharing strategy of a library may enable:
   (a) Shared use
   (b) Exchange of materials
   (c) Joint Acquisition
   (d) All of the above

Ans. : 192. (a) 193. (a) 194. (b) 195. (a) 196. (c) 197. (a) 198. (d) 199. (c) 200. (d)

201. Andrew Carnegie was a Library Scientist.
   (a) True (b) False

202. The 'Study Aboard' is a/an:
   (a) Directory (b) Year Book
   (c) Hand Book (d) Encyclopedia

203. Special Library Association (SLA) is situated in:
   (a) Chicago (b) New York
   (c) Washington (d) Paris

204. Calcutta Public Library was established in:
   (a) 1836 (b) 1846
   (c) 1856 (d) 1867

205. Andhra Pradesh Library Association was established in the year:
   (a) 1905 (b) 1908
   (c) 1914 (d) 1917

206. The first chairman of U. G. C. (India) was:
   (a) C. D. Deshmukh (b) S. R. Ranganathan
   (c) S. Radhakrishanan (d) None of the above

207. In which year the first School of Library Science was started in UK:
   (a) 1904 (b) 1911
   (c) 1919 (d) 1921

208. ....celebrated as World Book & copyright Day:
   (a) 1st April (b) 11th April
   (c) 23rd April (d) 30th April

209. Government of India Libraries Association (GILA) was formed at Imperial Secretariat, Shimla in:
   (a) 1932 (b) 1933
   (c) 1935 (d) 1936

Ans. : 201. (b) 202. (c) 203. (b) 204. (a) 205. (c) 206. (a) 207. (d) 208. (c) 209. (b)

210. Which of the following years mark the advent of free and tax supported public library system in U.K.:

(a) 1756 (b) 1850

(c) 1866 (d) 1956

211. The Committee on 'Structural of Pubic Library Services in England and Wales' is also known as:

(a) Kenyon committee (b) Parry committee

(c) Edwards committee (d) Roberts committee

212. Abbreviation LIBER stands for:

(a) European Research Libraries

(b) Library and Education & Research

(c) Libraries for Education and Research

(d) None of the above

213. Indian National Digital Library in Science and Technology is also known as:

(a) INDLST (b) IATUL

(c) INDEST (d) INDLIST

214. Indian Institute of Technology, Madras (IITM) was established in 1959 by the Government of India, as an institute of national importance.

(a) True (b) False

215. Abbreviation SIS stands for:

(a) Science for Information Science

(b) Indian Science Society

(c) Information for Social Science

(d) Society for Information Science

216. SIS is located in:

(a) Orissa (b) New Delhi

(c) Kolkata (d) Ahmedabad

Ans. :

210. (b)	211. (d)	212. (a)	213. (c)
214. (a)	215. (d)	216. (b)	

217. Commonwealth Educational Media Centre for the Asia (CEMCA) was founded in 1987 by the Commonwealth Heads of Government at their meeting Vancouur, Canada.

(a) True (b) False

218. Society for Information Science (SIS) was setup in New Delhi in the year:

(a) 1966 (b) 1972
(c) 1976 (d) 1982

219. Melvil Dewey was related to:

(a) France (b) USA
(c) UK (d) Brazil

220. Seymour Lubetzky is related with his contribution in the field of:

(a) Documentation (b) Management
(c) Cataloguing (d) Computer Science

221. Universal Copyright convention of 1952 was held in:

(a) Paris (b) Geneva
(c) New York (d) The Hauge

222. The most recent library act was passed by which of the following states:

(a) Bihar (b) Pondicherry
(c) Uttar Pradesh (d) Goa

223. Head Quarter of ILA is moved from Calcutta to Delhi in:

(a) 1932 (b) 1933
(c) 1963 (d) 1964

224. How many books were published by Dr. S. R. Ranganathan?

(a) 62 (b) 64
(c) 67 (d) 69

Ans. :

217. (a)	218. (c)	219. (b)	220. (c)
221. (b)	222. (b)	223. (d)	224. (a)

225. Who called Ranganathan's era as 'Age of Ranganathan':

(a) M, Dewey
(b) W. C. B. Sayers
(c) S. Radhakrishanan
(d) A. V. Dickinson

226. Dr. S. R. Ranganthan was founder of:

(a) AGLIS
(b) IASLIC
(c) ABGILA
(d) SLA

227. The Zoological Society of India was established in:

(a) 1834
(b) 1894
(c) 1939
(d) 1944

228. Botanical Survey of India was established in..................in Calcutta:

(a) 1834
(b) 1839
(c) 1934
(d) 1989

229. The theory X and Y appeared in:

(a) 1960
(b) 1966
(c) 1970
(d) 1972

230. 'The Good Society' is written by:

(a) P. Rafter
(b) R. Bellah
(c) Peter F. Drucker
(d) Peter Martin

231. Copyright law has passed by American Govt. in:

(a) 1897
(b) 1945
(c) 1970
(d) 1870

232. Other name of book ends is:

(a) Book Support
(b) Book Finish
(c) Last Book
(d) All the above

233. Who was the pioneer of the open access system in the British people libraries:

(a) H. E. Bliss
(b) John Cotton Dana
(c) Nina Browne
(d) J. D. Brown

Ans. : 225. (b) 226. (c) 227. (c) 228. (b) 229. (a) 230. (b) 231. (d) 232. (a) 233. (d)

234. 'Ranga' is the nickname of:
   (a) Ranga C. N. (b) Ranganathan
   (c) C. N. Ranga (d) None of the above

235. Who is a bibliothecar?
   (a) Author of Articles (b) Translator
   (c) Librarian (d) Computer Operator

236. National Library India inaugurated on:
   (a) 1st Feb., 1948 (b) 1st Feb., 1963
   (c) 1st Feb., 1954 (d) 1st Feb., 1956

237. Dr. S. R. Ranganathan lived in Zurich from 1955 to ....:
   (a) 1956 (b) 1957
   (c) 1958 (d) 1959

238. What position did Ranganathan hold with the MALA:
   (a) Secretary (b) Dy-secretary
   (c) President (d) Vice-President

239. Who was the librarian of the Imperial Library at Delhi, during the resign of Jalaludin Khilji:
   (a) Babur (b) Firdusi
   (c) Fakir Ahmed (d) Amir Khusrau

240. First Mobile Library was started in the state of:
   (a) Delhi (b) Andhra Pradesh
   (c) Tamil Nadu (d) Bihar

241. Index Society of the U.K. was founded in year:
   (a) 1877 (b) 1895
   (c) 1905 (d) 1907

Ans. :

234. (b)	235. (c)	236. (b)	237. (b)
238. (a)	239. (d)	240. (c)	241. (a)

242. E. W. Hulme was the librarian of:
   (a) Imperial Library, India
   (b) Patent Office Library, Paris
   (c) Patent Office Library, London
   (d) British Library, London

243. Which is not barrier in Library Resource Sharing:
   (a) Cumbersome library procedures
   (b) Predetermined terms and conditions
   (c) Rivalries between parent bodies
   (d) Inadequate library collection

244. ILL stands for:
   (a) Indian Library Loan
   (b) Index of Library Loan
   (c) Informatics Library Loan
   (d) Inter Library Loan

245. Story hours, Exhibitions and reading to illiterate are forms of:
   (a) Reference Service (b) Extension Service
   (c) Special Service (d) All of the above

Ans. : 242. (c) 243. (b) 244. (d) 245. (b)